THE CATECHISM OF THE CATHOLIC CHURCH: *Familystyle*

We Celebrate

VOLUME 2

David M. Thomas, Ph.D.
& Mary Joyce Calnan

ThomasMore®
A DIVISION OF TABOR PUBLISHING

Allen, Texas

NIHIL OBSTAT
Reverend Edward L. Maginnis, S.J.
Censor Deputatus

IMPRIMATUR
Very Rev. Donald F. Dunn
Vicar General for the Diocese
 of Colorado Springs

October 5, 1994

The nihil obstat and imprimatur are official declarations that a book or pamphlet is free of doctrinal or moral error. No implication is contained therein that those have granted the nihil obstat and the imprimatur agree with the content, opinion, or statements expressed.

ACKNOWLEDGMENTS

Scripture quotations are taken from or adapted from the Good News Bible text, Today's English Version. Copyright © American Bible Society 1966, 1971, 1976, 1993.

Excerpts from the English translation of the *Catechism of the Catholic Church for the United States of America,* copyright © 1994, United States Catholic Conference, Inc.—Liberia Editrice Vaticana.

DESIGN: Davidson Design

Send all inquiries to:
Thomas More Publishing
200 East Bethany Drive
Allen, Texas 75002–3804

Printed in the United States of America

ISBN 0–88347–296–1

2 3 4 5 6   00 99 98 97 96

Contents

It is the tradition of families to hand down their most treasured possessions from one generation to the next. Each new generation accepts the special gift with great reverence, because it connects the family with its history, identity, values, and stories.

It is in this tradition that the family which is the Church has treasured the gift of faith and the inheritance that the Creator bestows on us as the children of God. The gift of faith has been treasured and preserved down through the ages in the stories of Scripture, the teachings of the Church, the writings of saints and scholars, the celebrations of sacramental life, and the witness of lives of love and service.

In this spirit, our Holy Father Pope John Paul II convoked an extraordinary assembly of the Synod of Bishops in 1985 which began the task of drafting a compendium of Catholic doctrine to insure that the inheritance of our faith story, values, and traditions would be accessible to and suited for the generations of the present and the future. The *Catechism of the Catholic Church* is primarily a resource of doctrinal, moral, social, and spiritual teaching for all those who have been given the responsibility of passing on our faith inheritance.

David Thomas and Mary Joyce Calnan have taken the *Catechism* down from the shelf, as it were, have given it life, and have made it an inheritance that will be passed down from family to family, from generation to generation. Their four-volume *Catechism of the Catholic Church: Familystyle* is the first local or national catechism written from the original resource. They are faithful and careful stewards of the Church's treasure of faith and values. First, they have divided their familystyle catechism into the same divisions as the *Catechism of the Catholic Church*—Creed, Sacraments,

Life in Christ, and Prayer. Second, the reader can follow the development of topics in the same order as the new *Catechism*. Third, they connect the doctrine of our faith to the reality of life today in a process and style that touches your heart and your spirit. By adapting the *Catechism* to the culture and lifestyle of the family, they "unwrap" the *Catechism* and allow us to know our God as intimately caring and as connected to our everyday lives.

David and Mary Joyce are exemplary disciples of the Master Teacher as they skillfully and sensitively tell extraordinary stories of ordinary people, which draw you into the Word of God in Scripture and into the particular teaching of our faith tradition. Each chapter invites the reader to reflect on story, Scripture, doctrine and then to apply this to his or her own life as a family member. Each chapter concludes with a prayer for the rich resource of Church tradition adapted to the language and life of the family. Although this resource is intended primarily for families in all the many shapes and forms of family systems today, I believe that *The Catechism of the Catholic Church: Familystyle* will be a special gift to everyone in catechetical, liturgical, and other pastoral ministries as a resource and as a spiritual companion.

I am deeply honored to be invited to write the foreword for this book. David Thomas and Mary Joyce Calnan have a rich background in family life ministry. Their *Catechism of the Catholic Church: Familystyle* reflects that ministry as this work brings faith to life and life to faith. I know that readers will join with me in expressing my deepest gratitude for this gift of faith and love that will undoubtedly become a new classic in American Catholic spirituality.

Howard J. Hubbard
Bishop of Albany, NY

Introduction

You have just opened *We Celebrate,* the second book in a four-volume series. This volume focuses on the seven sacraments of the Church and builds on *We Believe,* the first volume of the series. The four volumes of this familystyle catechism correspond to the four parts of the *Catechism of the Catholic Church* recently issued by the Vatican.

Pope John Paul II requested that the catechism of the whole Church be adapted to local churches. In *We Celebrate* we connect the life of the family with part two of the Vatican's catechism, "The Celebration of the Christian Mystery."

The nearness of our God is particularly evident when we reflect on the meaning of the sacraments in our faith life. God's love for the world is so great that the Son of God, Jesus, lived right here on earth with us. God continues to live with us in the earthy, sacramental life of the Church.

When Catholics think of "sacrament," we usually think of the seven sacraments of the Church. It is an interesting historical footnote that the identification and naming of the "seven" came almost 1,500 years after the birth of Jesus. History teaches that the Church's understanding of "sacrament" has evolved and enjoys a rich and varied history.

At this moment in the history of the Church, particular attention is being paid to the importance of everyone's *participation* in the sacramental rituals of the gathered parish community. Sacramental moments are times to be active, not passive.

In this volume we will look at the sacramental life of the Church through the lens of family—sacramentality in action. It is somewhat like the excitement that comes during a search—a quest—for buried treasure. We know that God is present in families. Our quest is to recognize the reality of our God in the midst of the reality of family.

Let us begin.

CHAPTER ONE
God Hidden and Present in Creation

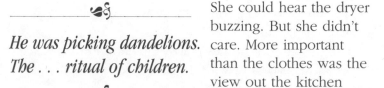

He was picking dandelions. The . . . ritual of children.

She could hear the dryer buzzing. But she didn't care. More important than the clothes was the view out the kitchen window to the yard that badly needed mowing. What she was looking at was her two-year-old.

The little guy was knee-deep in long grass . . . yes, but that was only a part of the beauty of what she saw. Red shorts bulging with diapers. Her older child's old shirt stained with every kind of jelly and gelatin made. A head of curly hair just like that on the man she'd married. Little chubby legs, scratched and bruised from his busy life.

But what held her there, looking out into her familiar world of the backyard, was what this little person was doing.

He was picking dandelions. The all-American ritual of children. Making a bouquet . . . of the easiest flower she'd ever been able to grow!

Twirling around, frequently falling flat on his rump, sometimes gaining upright posture to scan the horizon for better specimens . . . yet, always, always holding steadfast to the drooping contents in his chubby hands.

"Oh, Lord, what a sight," she said out loud to herself. "Nothing in the world compares to what I'm seeing right now."

She couldn't help herself. She went out onto the patio to await the holy delivery.

He finished his careful picking and the difficult task of adding each flower to his now crowded little hand.

Then, like a grown-up who'd just harvested the best in the garden, he started for the house. Spotting her on the patio, he began to sprint through the knee-deep grass.

She knew he'd fall but reluctantly held back so as not to ruin his surprise.

Fall he did, but he never lost his handful of joy. Fixed on his goal and with a grin broader than his little face, he darted for his mother.

Bending down to greet him and receive his blessed offering, she suddenly realized tears were streaming down her face.

"Mommy, I picked some flowers for you," the child said.

She couldn't help but think that this was the reason for dandelions.

> *"From the beginning until the end of time the whole of God's work is a blessing."*
>
> CCC, 1079

As Jesus was coming near Jericho, there was a blind man sitting by the road, begging. When he heard the crowd passing by, he asked, "What is this?"

"Jesus of Nazareth is passing by," they told him.

He cried out, "Jesus! Son of David! Have mercy on me!"

The people in front scolded him and told him to be quiet. But he shouted even more loudly, "Son of David! Have mercy on me!"

So Jesus stopped and ordered the blind man to be brought to him. When he came near, Jesus asked him, "What do you want me to do for you?"

"Sir," he answered, "I want to see again."

Jesus said to him, "Then see! Your faith has made you well."

At once he was able to see, and he followed Jesus, giving thanks to God. When the crowd saw it, they all praised God.

Luke 18:35–43

The blind man gives glory to God through Jesus . . .

We live in a time and a culture in which we are always receiving signals. Information is always coming our way, information that means we must do something, respond, take action: dryers buzz, coupons offer us free bargains, phones ring, oven timers signal cookies ready for hungry mouths, and answering machines flash to tell us someone has called. Everywhere we turn we see signals, and we've learned that ignoring a signal might mean we'll miss out! So we pay attention and then decide to act or not.

That's what's happening in the story from Luke's Gospel. The day is probably hot and dusty. The blind man could've been sitting by the roadside since early morning, just listening and hoping for signals of the approach of someone who might give him something— money, food, kindness. This is the only way he can survive.

Then he hears the crowd, signaling something's happening. He can only hear; he can't see who's coming down the road; others must be his eyes. They tell him, with great gladness, that Jesus of Nazareth is passing by.

Here is the signal. And this signal calls forth his openness to Jesus and Jesus' message of God's quickening love. Quickly, very quickly, the blind man must act.

Of course, Jesus, moved to compassion, heals the man. But more than healing is significant here. The blind man has faith in Jesus' presence. Even before his eyes can see, the blind man, with faith, "sees" and recognizes the signal of Jesus' great goodness. The blind man gives glory to God through Jesus, then rises up, and follows him.

The young mother in our opening story sits along the roadway, too, so to speak. And then her precious child and his gathering of dandelions signals to her, invites her to see the presence of God in her ordinary day. And because she is open, the gift of God's loving touch blesses her. This blessing comes both in her child and in the beauty of the reason for dandelions.

God's first message to us is "It's okay to be human."

God, our Creator, always relates to us as humans: Because we are made from matter, God uses matter to communicate with us. We understand what we see through our senses—touch, seeing, hearing, taste, and smell. If we don't use our senses, we do not truly know ("see") who and what is with us.

Because we are social beings, God communicates to us as a community. God loves us. And God shows this love by never asking us to do what we cannot do; God does not expect us to know that which we cannot know or to see that which we cannot see.

Sensitive adults don't ask young children to solve complex math problems. Sensitive spouses don't expect perfection of each other in all ways. Yet we can have hopes and expectations of each other and ourselves. Of course, these hopes and expectations must be realistic or we become frustrated and angry, not pleasant to be around.

God is the supreme realist! God's first message to us is "It's okay to be human. I spent a lot of care in creating you, and I like you just as you are. You will please yourself and me if you celebrate and give thanks just for being human." Thus, the young mother in our story experiences a very human reality—her child gathering flowers. And this act is a blessing for her.

God as hidden yet there

A game infants love is "peekaboo." No one knows who invented it. There is no "Peekaboo Hall of Fame." What's also interesting is that almost every culture in the world has a version of this game. The game seems to have something to do with being human, and it has real importance for infants. For all of us, peekaboo is connected with the growing-up process. This game we play with babies is about trust and letting go and believing in things not seen.

Let's recall the rules: The caregiver stands within the infant's field of vision. The infant spontaneously smiles. The adult moves her or his face and hides it from the infant. This confuses the baby, who sometimes begins to be afraid. However, the familiar face reappears in the infant's sight, and the baby smiles an even bigger smile than before. The world is good; we can trust it.

From the standpoint of parents, the game is great. Parents need no special equipment; they can play peekaboo anywhere—indoors or outside. They don't have to spend hours assembling the parts; they don't have to make a special trip to the hardware store to buy batteries! And infants seem to have an unlimited interest in the game. In all of recorded history, no infant ever grew tired of the game. (So we hear.) Parents, however, have been known to reach their limit after two or three peekaboos!

Why does this seemingly simple game enthrall infants?

When we first come into the world, a cord connects us to what's already there. Once someone severs the cord, we remain connected to others through our physical senses, especially through touch and sight. Everything seems fine to us as long as we remain connected with those we care about. Panic sets in when we sense that we might be alone—that is, without familiar humans.

> *The baby smiles an even bigger smile than before. The world is good.*

One of the first questions we ask is directly connected with our first experiences of being alone. The question is simply, Are we alone? We are so young when we first ask this basic question that none of us really remembers the answer we gave ourselves or received from another. But we did receive some answer that first time. Throughout our lives, we continue to ask this question in various forms. In truth, it is among the most important questions we ever ask. And the question is related to peekaboo.

What lesson does this game teach the infant? It's obvious. The familiar adult is there whether seen or not. An important lesson.

Seeing God who is hidden

Changing the characters in the game, can we say the same thing about God? Is God here for us even when we do not sense the presence of God? As humans, we all know that God is Spirit, which simply means that God is not material, not made of matter. However, God does create matter. Is God's presence in this matter?

Is there a knothole in the fence of creation through which we can peek and see this loving God in action?

We believe that God is always present in creation, holding dear the universe and we who are in it, thinking about us, loving us, cherishing us. But can we see God, our Creator? Is there a knothole in the fence of creation through which we can peek and see this loving God in action?

Yes.

Let's recall what Jesus said during the Last Supper.. His disciples asked him to show them the Father. Jesus answered that when they see him, Jesus, they are seeing the Father. This is at least part of the Christian answer to the question, Can we see God? We can, if we look to Jesus.

And because Jesus continues to live and remain active in the life of the Church, we can also look there to see God. But our seeing is always through our senses. So, we see through created reality, through something God has made.

Contemplating the magnificence of creation itself or the human works of creation can lead us to perceive something of the wisdom and beauty of God the Creator. This kind of human reflection has filled Christians and others with deep wonder about the graciousness of our God.

God as the mystery of love

When we love we are as God is.

Thus far, we have affirmed that God is present in all creation; God sustains creation through divine creative power; and the power of God, as manifested through all God's actions, is the power/energy of love.

Power not connected with love can easily be destructive or unreliable. The wind blows one way today, the other way tomorrow. We cannot trust it. Is God's power like that? No. We *can* trust in God's power because it is always an expression of God's love. God's love for each and all of us.

God is a God of life. The creation of the entire universe almost 15 billion years ago was geared toward the eventual creation of that life. And life reaches its highest, fullest level when we humans came to be. Why? Because we are created in the image of God. And when are humans most human? Again, the answer is simple and deep. When we love. That's when we are as God is.

Let's recall our reflections about God in Volume 1, *We Believe*. We talked about how we cannot separate genuine love from the presence of God. When love is present in our life, God is manifested there. We concluded that God was not only present in us but also between us in relationships. In the story of the toddler and his mother that begins this chapter, love is present between the mother and her child; God is present.

> *Whatever Jesus did, love motivated him.*

Jesus went about doing good, which means he loved people more than any of us who ever loved. And he acted on his love. Sometimes he helped others; sometimes he walked away. Sometimes he worked miracles in response to human needs like those of the blind man we read about earlier; sometimes he seemed to let things stand. Nevertheless, whatever Jesus did, love motivated him.

When we truly love, freely and unconditionally, we see more deeply. We take time to wonder, to gaze out the window, to look again and again. In fact, when we really love in the way God intends us to love, we may even be able to see, know, and feel God.

This mystery, which lies at the deepest point in the created universe, deep in the earth, and high up in the vast array of other planets and stars, is the presence and the love of God. And no matter where we turn, we eventually find this love. All we need is the desire to find it and the belief that God's presence is with us.

The whole universe gives us the opportunity to become aware of God's loving presence. The abiding love of God sustains this universe, which came from the creative power of God. Daily, we need to stop, look, and listen as the mother did in our opening story.

We must find the deep center of ourselves where God dwells and listen to the symphony of God in the stillness of the night and in the activity of the day.

"The harmony of signs (songs, music, words, and actions) is all the more expressive and fruitful when expressed in the cultural richness *of the People of God who celebrate."*

CCC, 1158

Dandelions are the pioneers of the world of wildflowers!

For many, dandelions are weeds—the only good dandelion is a dead one! And we never seem to be able to get rid of them! We clear our own backyard, but dandelion seeds, millions of them, become airborne with the slightest breeze. They land everywhere, but they prefer landing in green yards that boast no yellow dots! Dandelions are the pioneers of the world of wildflowers!

Through the eyes of the mom in our opening story, we learn something about dandelions. They can become the most beautiful flower in all creation when an act of love harvests them.

But we have to see them in a special way.

Let's try to imagine what the blind man in our gospel story saw. The man had been blind from birth so he had never seen anything at all. What did he see in that first moment when Jesus removed the blindness from his eyes? What flood of light, colors, shapes?

Did the joy of sight excite the man so much that he had difficulty sleeping that first night? Did he shout "Look! Look at the stars! Look! Look at the moon! The shadows in the courtyard! The light dancing on the water!" To close his eyes was to end the show of incredible wonders. Yet eventually he must have slept. Then, what color-filled dreams he must have dreamt!

Our appreciation of the universe begins with wonder, with looking, with allowing the outside to enter the inside. The mom let the beautiful yellow bouquet enter her heart. These dandelions were not weeds; they were a gift from her son. And in her son dwelt the love of God. She welcomed the gift and no one could convince her ever again that dandelions were mere weeds. As Gerard Manley Hopkins, the Jesuit poet, said, "The world is charged with the grandeur of God."

No one should think that a perception like that of Hopkins or the toddler's mother or the man given sight by Jesus comes easy. To see beyond the surface of things, to go deeper than what appears, is a difficult human task. To find God in creation, we must look with the eyes of faith.

Through faith we open ourselves to the presence and communication of God anywhere, at any time, from anyone. A strong belief in God's presence in creation alerts us to be ready for the surprising appearance of God even in the most unlikely of places—places like dandelions in an overgrown yard, like a dusty roadside on the way to Jericho, like the hectic preparation of a family meal!

But the childlike quality of wonder starts the process of finding the world charged with God's presence. If we enter a new situation already in full possession of what we think we will see, we see no more than the obvious. We miss all that is there, and what's even sadder, we think that we have seen all there is to see. We miss everything that is hidden, mysterious, wonder-filled.

What do you see every day? Yourself in the morning mirror? Your same old family around the breakfast table? Your neighbors with their noisy dog? Streets, buildings, trees, sky? Pretty routine stuff.

Ordinary matters. And would all of this look any different if you knew that one minute later you would never ever see any of it again?

"In its earthly state the Church needs places where the community can gather together. Our visible churches, holy places, are images of the holy city . . . toward which we are making our way. . . ."

CCC, 1198

A Psalm

Happy are those who have the God of Jacob to help them / and who depend on the Lord their God, / the Creator of heaven, earth, and sea, / and all that is in them. / God always keeps promises; / and judges in favor of the oppressed / and gives food to the hungry. / The Lord God sets prisoners free and gives sight to the blind. / God lifts those who have fallen; / and loves righteous people. / God protects the strangers who live in our land; / helps widows and orphans, / but takes the wicked to their ruin. / The Lord God is king forever. / Your God, O Zion, will reign for all time. / Praise the Lord! *From Psalm 146:5–10*

Heart Sight

t is in those moments, O God,
When we sit by the roadway while living
our everyday life
That we perhaps miss the most.
Help us to listen carefully for your footsteps
into our hearts—
Footsteps that come from almost anywhere—
So that when we turn to see who comes,
we recognize it is you.
In the times when we're too tired to go on,
To solve one more problem,
Or work one more day,
Make one more bed,
Empty one more trash can,
Plan one more supper,
Or ask one more person for help.
Or other times to recognize it's you, too, we neglect
When we feed only ourselves and not the hungry,
Or ignore injustice,
Or bring harm to your environment,
Or don't hear the cries of others along the road
Who ask for you in our presence.
Help us to see, dear God. Really see.
Amen.

CHAPTER TWO
Celebrating Life's Major Moments with God

. . . the older mother was invited into the holy stable . . .

Her daughter had been in labor for over twenty-four hours. And, like many contemporary couples, her daughter and son-in-law said they'd call when the baby was born.

Nonetheless, she was worried sick. Surely by now the baby should have been born. It was after 4:00 A.M.!

"Oh, God, I hope everything's all right," she prayed.

Her own house was quiet with the silence of deep nighttime. The worry intensified since she had no one to talk to. (Except God, of course. God was always there.) But this was one of those times when she needed a human voice and human assurance.

To complicate things, the radio blurred out a warning about a dangerous ice storm that would arrive by dawn. Her maternal instincts told her to just go to the hospital. But other feelings interjected—based on the fact the two young people wanted to do this alone.

But instinct won out. The fifteen-minute trip took an hour on this winter night. Once inside the hospital, away from the cold and snow, she uncomfortably approached the birthing room.

When she peeked around the corner to see her daughter, the other feelings welled up again. She shouldn't have come. Birth had not happened yet, and at once she was sorry to have intruded into their sacred space.

Yet, her fears were important And she felt better. Her own child was safe—although still in the throes of creation's painful, life-giving dance.

Then the grandmother-to-be retreated to a waiting room far at the other end of the hall. "Stay out of their way," she told herself. "They want to do this alone. It'll be soon."

But hours passed. At times the older mother was invited into the holy stable by the father-to-be. Often she lingered nearby, listening and showing concern, yet honoring the sacred wish of the parents-to-be.

Then late in the day, near evening, she heard the blessed cry. She turned to rejoice . . . to someone (anyone!) in the hallway. But no one was there.

Until God entered.

For there, rounding a corner, were her son-in-law's parents. No longer able to await the news, they, too, gave in to parental instinct. Together the three grandparents heard their new grandchild's healthy cry and embraced, in holy celebration and in vast relief.

Then the door opened, and the new father came out. The look on his face was all she needed. Everything else was worth that moment . . . to see the face of someone who had just seen God.

There were some shepherds in that part of the
country who were spending the night in the fields,
taking care of their flocks. An angel of the Lord
appeared to them, and the glory of the Lord shone
over them. They were terribly afraid, but the angel
said to them, "Don't be afraid! I am here with good
news for you, which will bring great joy to all the
people."

When the angels went away from them back into
heaven, the shepherds said to one another, "Let's go
to Bethlehem and see this thing that has happened,
which the Lord has told us."

So they hurried off and found Mary and Joseph
and saw the baby lying in the manger. When the
shepherds saw him, they told them what the angel
had said about the child. All who heard it were
amazed at what the shepherds said. Mary remembered all these things and thought deeply about
them. The shepherds went back, singing praises to
God for all they had heard and seen; it had been
just as the angel had told them.

Luke 2:8–10, 15–20

*Simple human beings
announced God's coming.*

In ancient days, a
shepherd probably had a
lot in common with a
mother-in-law today: They
were persons with not-
too-favorable reputations;
staying away from them was the smart thing to do; and
no one ever wanted to end up being one!

However, ordinary life being what it is, both
shepherds and mothers-in-law, for the most part, are just
people bearing the burden of somebody else's actions!

Certainly not all shepherds were smelly, dirty, and uneducated. And not all mothers-in-law are bossy and nosy. Most (both shepherds and mothers-in-law) are special.

That the shepherds were the first human beings to hear the good news of Jesus' birth is of great significance. This birth fulfilled a promise God had made many, many years before. (And God always keeps promises!)

God, in keeping with who God is, decided to announce this great event through the most unlikely human beings—shepherds. They were to tell the rest of the human race! The message that Jesus was with us came from these lowly dregs of society. Simple human beings announced God's coming. And their news of great joy changed us forever.

In our opening story, the mother/grandmother (alias, mother-in-law) lingers near her flock. And in God's time, the child comes, and the news needs to be revealed. And so, in "Godstyle," God's presence appears when she most needs it, when she wants to celebrate the sacred moment with another human being. And what does God do? Of course, God provides yet another mother and father, the other grandparents (alias: in-laws). God knows what God is doing.

> *"The mystery of Christ is so unfathomably rich that it cannot be exhausted by . . . any single liturgical tradition."* CCC, 1201

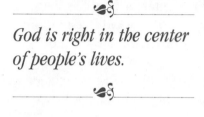

God is right in the center of people's lives.

Sometimes life's like a roller coaster, filled with ups and downs. Or sometimes it's like bumper cars with our car being the slowest to react. But then sometimes it's also like a smooth ride in a canoe, gentle movement accompanied by the soothing sound of rippling water.

Two bookends—our birth and our death—hold our lifetime together. In between these two events come others of greater or lesser importance. We sometimes call these events "rites of passage." They are like mileposts along our journey. In our culture, for instance, the government and the family permit a sixteen-year-old to pilot the family vehicle down the interstate. Wheels! Freedom! Life—at last!

We remember these moments. And a family ritual (like the formal handing over of the car keys) often accompanies these events.

Religious rites or rituals are part of being human. The Church did not invent the use of rituals. What the Church did, however, and still does, is to observe the ordinary way people celebrate life and death and the various rites of passage. The Church then connected, and connects, these rites of passage with our faith.

Within these connections between being human and being a person of faith, we experience God. In Chapter One, we explored the wonderful realization that God did not disconnect from the world once the universe was set in motion. God is not blasé; God does not sit on a heavenly throne watching what happens while yawning over the tediousness of life. God is in the midst of things. God is vitally engrossed, ever and always, with each of us.

In fact, God is right in the center of people's lives. And to make this really evident to us, God lived among us as Jesus, who revealed and proclaimed both the presence and the power of God. From an infant lying on hay to an adult walking the dusty roads of Galilee, Jesus experienced the presence of God in all his own ups and downs.

Through our celebration of the sacraments, we experience God's presence in our own lives. The sacraments are open windows to our God. They give us a special opportunity to become aware of God's abiding presence. We have named seven sacraments. Each connects with a significant event, one of those major movement times of our lives, one of those times we can readily recognize our God. We must savor these seven sacramental moments, for they invite us to enter more deeply into the experience of our lives. They are not moments of escape from this world, but celebrations of this world—its past, present, and future. We must resist simply checking them off as things to do at a specific time in our life. No. They are moments in which we experience the presence of a God more wonderful than anyone we have ever known or dreamt of.

The sacraments are open windows to our God. They give us a special opportunity to become aware of God's abiding presence.

God's gentle touch

Some of us think that God zaps us with divine life when we receive a sacrament. We say some words, the celebrant performs some actions, and Zowey! We change into something new! We assume it's automatic. But our God doesn't work like that. God treats us always in relationship. As persons.

The wonderful scriptural story of the woman with a condition of chronic vaginal bleeding points to this. As usual, crowds gather around Jesus. Apparently the woman knows of his reputation as a healer, so she concludes that all she needs to do is touch the hem of his robe and she will be healed.

As the story goes, the woman touches his robe, and just as she expected, she is cured. All of a sudden, however, Jesus

Jesus asks, "Who touched me?" Making physical contact is not enough; the two personalities must connect.

stops everything and asks who touched him. He is very aware that his healing energy passed onto someone. But he also wants us to know that this doesn't just happen, so to speak, automatically. His robe is not magic.

The woman believes in Jesus' goodness, but her action is incomplete. To connect with the power of Jesus, she must connect with Jesus himself. She needs a personal encounter. Jesus asks, "Who touched me?" The "who" and the "me" are personal. Making physical contact is not enough; the two personalities must connect.

Sacraments are personal encounters between God and self. The external words and actions connect with internal attitudes and thoughts. It all forms one very important reality.

Liturgy—alive and inviting

The very first official document from Vatican II dealt with the liturgy of the Church. The word *liturgy* comes from a nonchurch word meaning "the work of the people." In the context of the Church, the word means the official public worship and prayer of the Church.

Vatican II emphasized two important ideas: (1) The official public worship and prayer of the Church must be intelligible to all. The language must be the language of the gathered people. The symbols used during the liturgy must communicate meaning to the community. And the connection between liturgical celebration and human life must be clear to those gathered, not just to those in charge.

(2) When the community gathers for liturgical celebrations, everyone is to be involved. The liturgy has no room for passive observers or silent listeners. We enter liturgy to become active, alive, and totally involved. While this invitation carries an idealistic tone, it remains as an important part of the sacramental life of the Church. The ideal is particularly challenging in places where the majority of the people are accustomed to being passive participants, where they "go to church" instead of gathering "as church."

When our days and nights are devoid of rituals or celebration, we run the danger of making life flat.

The actions and words used within the liturgy are very important. These outward symbols touch our senses and signify what is happening inwardly.

The way we celebrate liturgy is the way we believe. Both in this familystyle catechism and in the larger catechism belief and celebration are connected as the first and second parts. They are positioned next to each other because that is the way they are related.

When our days and nights are devoid of rituals or celebration, we run the danger of making life flat. Boredom sets in and routine dominates. Celebrations connect us with power and energy. Celebrations bring a contrast between the special and the ordinary. Ordinary is important, but when it's all we have, life becomes somewhat boring. And life isn't. Life is a miracle happening every moment.

Our Catholic beliefs center on God's great generosity in creating us and redeeming us. Often Scripture uses the image of a banquet to remind us of what has happened and is happening right now.

In the Gospel, or good news, according to John, the first sign of the kingdom is the wedding feast at Cana. The feast was probably typical for its time—a celebration with people and music and food and drink. People were enjoying themselves.

At this feast in Cana, something terrible happened. The people, music, and food held out, but the drink didn't. A social faux pas was in the making!

> *So Mary gave Jesus the look that mothers of firstborns have used for centuries.*

The mother of Jesus, always sensitive to the needs of others, was among the first to notice the empty jars and the look on the faces of the couple who wanted their friends to have a good time. Something had to be done. After all, she may have thought, weddings are special times, because they celebrate love's always surprising abundance.

So Mary gave Jesus the look that mothers of first-borns have used for centuries. She then turned to the servants and advised them to do what her son asked. We know the rest of the story. Water into wine; ordinary into extraordinary; scarcity into abundance. Jesus' first miracle. The kingdom had begun.

*"The mystery of Christ is so
unfathomably rich that it
cannot be exhausted by its
expression in any single
liturgical tradition.*

*"Through the liturgical life
of a local church, Christ, the
light and salvation of all peoples,
is made manifest to the
particular people and culture
to which that Church is sent and
in which she is rooted."*

CCC, 1201, 1202

We could call these moments . . . the family's liturgy.

The family has a life cycle, just as each person has a life cycle. Each and every family goes through certain predictable stages. Because families never really begin nor end; we can never undo being a family, no matter how hard we try. In one way or another, family stays with us biologically, psychologically, spiritually, and emotionally throughout our lifetime. We can try to leave the family behind, but family members travel with us in the way we are and in the way we live our lives, consciously or not.

One of the great indicators of a family's life cycle is the special moments when a family moves from one stage to another. What are some examples? The birth of the first child, the puberty of the first teenager, the last child leaving home. Each rite of passage calls forth from the family many mixed emotions.

As long as people live together and grow, families change. We celebrate some of these changing moments. When a baby is about to be born, we get the crib ready. Someone buys a special blanket or quilts one; friends buy diapers and bottles and rattles and tiny clothes. And when the baby comes—joy of joy!—people rush to welcome the new family member.

Other moments in our life just sort of come, as when someone has to take care of elderly parents. But no matter how these moments happen, they are an important part of our lives. And they are the sacramental moments of our family. These moments represent times when our lives are changing. We experience a passage, a momentous time. Clearly, God's presence is at work with us and in us and for us.

If we were to think about the most meaningful times with our family, these moments of passage would immediately come to mind. Some of us would name special vacations, birthdays, anniversaries, or other moments set aside to be together. Someone turned ten! Someone graduated! We won the championship Little League game! We burned the paid-up mortgage on the house! During these family "sacramental" moments, we came together to celebrate a deeper meaning in our lives.

But we would also probably identify some ordinary family times, such as after-dinner talks or one-on-one basketball games or winter fun or the kids' bedtime. In these ordinary, holy moments, we are conscious that we are present to one another. In these holy moments, our relationships are good, and for whatever reasons, our life problems and pains fade temporarily away. Then we can just be family. During these moments, our God is evident in our relationships. Our love thrives.

We could call these moments (together with the thousands of other day-in and day-out activities that are part of our lives together) the family's "liturgy." During these moments of our daily life we do our stuff as family—the ordinary "work of the people." During these moments, we actively participate in one another's lives. And yes, during these moments we use the best symbols and signs and words and actions of our love—like grilled hamburgers, airborne footballs, family jokes, stories of Uncle Dan and Aunt Judy, and barbecue recipes.

The next time you are busy with ordinary family chores; the next time you share laughter or relax together, name that time as holy. Why? Because you are loving one another. Indeed, that time *is* holy. Claim it as such, for our God is right there working with you, having fun, or even simply relaxing!

"The celebration of the liturgy, therefore, should correspond to the genius and culture of the different peoples. . . . It is with and through their own human culture, assumed and transfigured by Christ, that the multitude of God's children has access to the Father. . . ."

CCC, 1204

A Psalm

Lord, you have examined me and you know me. / You know everything I do; / from far away you understand all my thoughts. / You see me, whether I am working or resting; / you know all my actions. / Even before I speak, / you already know what I will say. / You are all around me on every side; / you protect me with your power. / Your knowledge of me is too deep; it is beyond my understanding.

You created every part of me; / you put me together in my mother's womb. . . .

Psalm 139:1–6,13

Our God Knits

 f God is a real God,
   Then we would expect God to do everything
      in a godly way,
      With strength and purpose,
Might and power,
And all that stuff.
So how is it that God
Is described as one who knits us together
Like a piece of cloth with many bright colors
Or a warm sweater with simple yarns?
Up close we may not appreciate the richness of design,
The carefully stitched parts,
The odd segments next to each other—
In seeming contrast
Clashing, crashing together.
Yet standing back,
Seeing it all in one eye,
It staggers us by its beauty.
A design only
Our God could imagine,
Only Love could
Wonderfully make.

CHAPTER THREE
Invitation to Live Fully

&5

The old man stood there . . . in that moment when soul meets soul.

&5

He lived alone, upstairs, on the third floor, where lots of the older men lived. He'd lived there for ages. He could barely remember any other place. This was home, even though he longed for a real home like he used to have with his family.

He spent his days out on the street, trying to find both food and a drink. Most days it was in the opposite order—first a drink and then food.

Sometimes, on hot days, he'd go to the park and watch the young families with little kids on the playground. Sometimes some of them even sat by the cement edge of the reflecting pool and watched the water. But rarely did anyone break the glasslike surface.

The man believed that hot people and cool water belonged together. "Something's the matter with not mixing the two!" he thought. "Signs or not, people and water go together!"

This day the old man noticed a little boy near the edge on the far side. He couldn't tell exactly what the child was doing, but he was on his stomach on the cement edge, with his head and hands over the side. He wandered around to see the unusual sight closer.

The child didn't move a muscle as the man neared. In fact, the old man thought perhaps something was wrong with the boy. So the man just stood next to him for a long time. The child remained still with his chin resting on the cement and his forehead and hands over the edge. The old man began to focus on the water in front of the child.

He saw the reflection of the child's face, and then his eyes. They were wandering, unfocused. The child was sensing the water; he was blind.

Hesitating in that moment when soul meets soul, longing to touch the water himself, he felt a union with the boy. Awe filled the old man as he realized that, despite not seeing and not touching, the child was experiencing the water anyway.

Without thinking about what he was about to do, the old man asked the child if he could sit beside him. The boy, having long ago known he had a visitor, responded with a nod of his head. The man sat down, then rolled onto his stomach like the child, at a comfortable distance.

Then he put his hands in the water and began to move them around. The boy, hearing the swish of the water, asked, "Is that okay? Can we put our hands in the water?"

"Yes, we can put our hands in the water," his older friend answered. "That's why it's here."

That's all it took. The child immediately laid his palms flat on the surface, gently touching the moist top, and then slowly forced them down, down, then sideways and back, and around, and out, and up, and then he began to splash. All over his friend and himself, he splashed.

The old man did the same. In no time, a grin came to the child's face, mirroring the face of his new friend. And the park was suddenly blessed with the laughter of two young boys playing.

After this, Jesus went to Jerusalem for a religious festival. Near the Sheep Gate in Jerusalem there is a pool with five porches; in Hebrew it is called Bethzatha. A large crowd of sick people were lying on the porches—the blind, the lame, and the paralyzed. A man was there who had been sick for thirty-eight years. Jesus saw him lying there, and he knew that the man had been sick for such a long time; so he asked him, "Do you want to get well?"

The sick man answered, "Sir, I don't have anyone here to put me in the pool when the water is stirred up; while I am trying to get in, somebody else gets there first."

Jesus said to him, "Get up, pick up your mat, and walk." Immediately the man got well; he picked up his mat and started walking.   *John 5:1–9*

_____ 🙌 _____

We often wait to be "put in the water". . .

_____ 🙌 _____

Our ancestors chose the stories they recorded in Scripture for good reasons. Obviously, the stories in the New Testament, which apply to life after the birth of Jesus, are just a small sampling of all the events of his life.

But, like the family stories in this book (bits and pieces from lives), the stories in the Scriptures are there for a good reason, often many reasons. The story above is one of those. In the story, the water heals, cleanses, and purifies; Jesus, through his questioning, invites the man to follow the good news of God's abiding concern and love; the man, cured of his thirty-eight-year afflic-tion, picks up his mat and begins to walk!

All these happenings are important. But the scenario—the sick or handicapped people at the water, the human nature of laws and restrictions (No Swimming!)—are all part of our lives. We often wait to be "put in the water," so to speak. Often we say something like "Jump in! Get your feet wet!" We're not really talking about water either; rather, we're talking about other aspects of our life.

As the little boy lay by the water in our opening story, he extended (all unknowingly) an invitation to his older friend who had just arrived in his life. How did the child offer this invitation? Simply by being at the pool at the right time. The elderly man extended an invitation too. Seeking a better life, he joined the child in like-to-like needs. And together, they symbolically found something new and wonderful. What? The freedom to refresh themselves in the healing water, the freedom to play.

Our God is like that. Waiting in the most unlikely places—as well as in the most likely. Just waiting for us to be open to the refreshment offered by our playful God.

> *"Since the beginning of the world, water, so humble and wonderful a creature, has been the source of life and fruitfulness."*
>
> CCC, 1218

At the top of God's list . . .
"Create water."

Every Christian starts with baptism. A watery entry. The sacrament is like the long history of the human race: We leave the sea and step onto dry land. Our human journey has begun. We walk and talk. And we always live next to that substance in the universe that is most essential to life—water. How far to the next watering hole? We can't go any farther than that. When earth dwellers left their home planet in search of life on the moon, what did they first look for? Water.

We cannot live without water. Without this necessary liquid, our bodies shrivel like a prune. So at the top of God's list of things to do when fashioning creation, we find the reminder, "Create water."

Our tradition of the sacraments stretches back to water stories in the New Testament and even beyond. The first water story in the Old Testament is right at its beginning. God, as an awesome wind, breathes over the darkened waters and creates light and the first day. (Once God has light, it is easier to work on subsequent days!) But the point is that all began with water. A new beginning in Scripture. Water is introduced to us.

The story of Noah is really a story of salvation. Water does not destroy everything, because God wants life to continue. So God preserves Noah and his family and two of every animal type. Endangerment gives way to salvation, hope and another new beginning. (Water.)

Later in the Old Testament we encounter the story of Moses. The pharaoh's sister finds Moses as an infant floating on the water. Some of us know the general outline of his water story. Moses and the Israelites pass through the waters of the Red Sea to freedom and new life. The water saves them for a new beginning. (Water.)

Jesus and water

Shortly after leaving home as an adult male, Jesus comes to the river Jordan. His cousin, John the Baptist, in accord with his own sense of what God wants of him, is baptizing people who have come to him to seek repentance.

John is a wild sort. (The Gospels describe him as living in the desert, eating honey and locusts, and dressed in a loincloth.) We may imagine him as a true eccentric. No matter. To Jesus he is kin. So as a special expression of family support, Jesus submits himself to the baptism that John offers.

Now Jesus is no sinner, but he seeks this baptism. Why? Perhaps because he is about to begin something new in his life. As Jesus wades to the riverbank after his baptism, the heavens open and a voice thunders forth, "You are my own dear Son. I am pleased with you" (Luke 3:22). And Jesus begins his new life of proclaiming the good

A woman with a rather unusual personal history comes to the well to draw some water. Jesus casually asks her for a drink.

news of God's extraordinary and ever-present love for us. He comes forth from the river. (Water.)

Later in the Scriptures, Jesus is in Samaria, stopping by a village well. A woman with a rather unusual personal history comes to the well to draw some water. Jesus casually asks her for a drink.

The request startles the woman, and what follows is one of the most interesting conversations recorded in the Gospels. (It's found in the fourth chapter of John's Gospel.) As their dialogue unfolds, Jesus informs the Samaritan woman that he can make available to her "living" waters. If she drinks these waters, Jesus says, she will never again be thirsty.

As the narrative ends, the woman realizes that Jesus is referring not to the water from the well, but to water that has something to do with himself, water that can give her a new beginning in life. (Water.)

At the death of Jesus, the Scriptures mention water again. This time, water flows from the wound in Jesus' chest, close to his heart. An end, and a beginning. (Water.)

The various water stories in the Scriptures contain certain common elements. They are connected with life, with new beginnings, with freedom, and with God's creative power. Most beginnings in the Scriptures will make some reference to water. That's because the Bible is about God's gift of life. And that's what the sacrament of Baptism is all about.

Baptism and the new creation

The Scriptures mention water on the first day of creation and on what we call the "eighth day," meaning the day of Jesus' resurrection, when God's plan for creation came to completion.

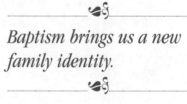

Baptism brings us a new family identity.

With the resurrection of Jesus something brand-new appears on earth, the Risen Christ. God has made new the humanity of Jesus. In the Risen Christ, God accomplishes the full and complete intent of creation. When God raises Jesus from death, Jesus acquires the fullness of life.

In the sacrament of Baptism, the power of God's Spirit gathers us into God and transforms us, giving us new life. The sacrament makes us members of the Church, family members. In baptism, we symbolically plunge into the water (which symbolizes the death of Jesus). Then we symbolically rise from the water, gasping for air (symbolizing our rising, as Jesus did,

to new life). We experience a new birth—a new life—
through the waters of baptism.

The celebrant administers baptism in the name of
the Triune God—the Father, Son, and Holy Spirit.
Created in the image of God, we are, in a sense, God's
own self-portrait. We reflect God. And that reflection is
most true when we live with and love others. In the
beginning, we alienated ourselves from God. But sin
was not the last word. The last word is God's. And this
final word is "Love." It is a word of acceptance, a word
of forgiveness. All this comes to be through the
sacrament of Baptism.

Baptism brings us home to God. The Church has
called our condition upon birth "original sin." We are
born into a world still in need of God's gift of grace—
a world in which evil also lives. God's gift of divine life,
called sanctifying grace (given through baptism), aids us
in overcoming the world's evil. Baptism gives us what
we need to live, a life of love.

Baptism, the sacrament of our salvation, is our entry
into the promised life. After the resurrection of Jesus, his
disciples announced to the world what had been
accomplished through his coming and through his death
and resurrection. Then they invited others to truly be a
part of that reality. When those listening accepted the
good news, the apostles baptized them and expected
those "made new by the power of God" to act in accord
with their new identity. Outsiders would recognize
them, Jesus said at the Last Supper, by the love they
showed one another.

Demanding? Yes. Exciting? Yes. Challenging? Yes.
Difficult? Yes. Possible? Yes. But only when helped by God.

Baptism brings us a new family identity. For us, holy
and sacred events are happening. In families, in neigh-
borhoods, in work places, and in places where we play

and enjoy life, we witness these events. Only now we know, through our faith, that this holiness will never end. God has given us living waters. And everything has changed. We now live in God and God lives in us. The waters bring life in abundance—for ever, and ever.

The baptism of infants

Most Catholics were baptized as infants. Parents, grandparents, godparents may remember the day. But, those who were baptized then know about our baptism only through the stories and

In short, baptism is a religious event for the family as well as for the individual being baptized.

pictures snapped by our proud relatives. And so we may ask an important question: If the sacrament of Baptism is so important, why not wait until we can participate in the ritual with understanding and awareness? Why not be baptized when we're older?

The Church encourages infant baptism for several reasons: (1) Infant baptism communicates our belief that God initiates everything! God loves us first; God makes the first move; God invites us to become a part of God's family. (Even before we say yes or no!) (2) Infant baptism also focuses on the family dimension of our life of faith. When a parent brings an infant to the Church community for baptism, the Church asks the parent, not the infant, what is sought. The Church asks the parent to make a profession, a public statement of personal faith.

And toward the end of the baptismal ritual, the Church asks those present (the family and the local Christian community) if they will support and nourish the faith life of the newly baptized. In short, baptism is a religious event for the family as well as for the individual being baptized. In infant baptism, the sacrament is almost totally a *family* event.

Does the sacrament "stick" when we are baptized as infants? Yes. Is it forever? Yes. If we don't use it, do we lose it? Not really. The sacrament of Baptism, according to the tradition of the Catholic Church, creates "an indelible mark" on our soul. This reality is with us forever.

(The concept of being marked comes from the ancient secular world of being established in a certain position in society. In the past, people wore marks so that others would address them properly. This is a good example of the Church taking something from society, and reinterpreting its meaning. In its explanation of baptism, the Church took the secular "mark" and made it into a spiritual mark that did not wear off.)

Thus we understand baptism as our entrance into the Christian life. Baptism says who we are and how we are to live our lives. This sacrament keeps on giving as we participate in all the other sacraments of the Church.

Vatican II made a final, very important point concerning the baptism of non-Catholics. All baptized Christians are part of or members of the church of Jesus. All are sisters and brothers in Christ. The same life of God flows through our spiritual veins.

We may belong to different Christian communities or denominations. However, much more unites us than separates us. This is important for families divided by so-called religious differences. Jesus wants us to be one. We directly violate the Gospels when we emphasize religious differences among Christians and not what unites us. The Body of Christ—all Christians—is one.

Baptism gives us a "family root" in the community . . .

Our journey with and toward our God begins long before our baptism. the Scriptures tell us that God knows us before we are born; in fact, God knows every hair on our heads. That's pretty detailed. That's pretty intimate. And so our journey begins with God's knowledge of us.

Our Christian journey with Christ Jesus begins with baptism. If we are baptized as infants, those who love us most choose to make a commitment to teach us the ways of Jesus. Later, we ourselves will make this commitment. In fact, we will make this commitment again and again as we struggle to live our baptismal call to follow Christ. That is, to love one another.

Our baptism is forever. Baptism gives us a "family root" in the community of those who believe. This wonderful ritual welcomes us into God's Christian family.

When we have our children baptized, we need to choose godparents (those who represent God's family) who live their lives as Catholic Christians. People who will stay around our children and be additional witnesses to the faith. To reinforce the significance, we can ask godparents to attend the baptismal preparation sessions with us. We are in this together! It is a family (community) event!

If you haven't seen your godchildren or "godadult" lately, you might consider doing so. You might consider that this is part of that love Jesus talked about at the Last Supper. How to make contact? A simple phone call, a card, a date for lunch. Any of these actions says, "I'm your godparent, and this is what part of that means." Doing this might not hurt at all. In fact, it just might make at least two people a little happier.

A Psalm

Praise the Lord, my soul! . . . / You have spread out the heavens like a tent / and built your home on the waters above. . . . / You make springs flow in the valleys, / and rivers run between the hills. / They provide water for the wild animals; / there the wild donkeys quench their thirst. / In the trees near by, / the birds make their nests and sing. / From the sky you send rain on the hills, / and the earth is filled with your blessings.

Psalm 104:1–3, 10–13

Of Tubs and Other Family Places

h God, we praise you because . . .
Tubs are wonderful life-giving places
for bodies and minds
To relax and refresh in your wondrous gift
Of getting wet and clean
At the same time!

And sprinklers are wonderful life-giving places
for bodies and minds
To relax and refresh in your wondrous gift
Of getting wet and cool and surprised
At the same time!

And fire hydrants are wonderful life-giving places
for bodies and minds
To relax and refresh in your wondrous gift
Of getting wet and cool and laughing
At the same time!

And swimming pools are wonderful life-giving places
for bodies and minds
To relax and refresh in your wondrous gift
Of getting wet and cool and having fun
At the same time!

We praise you for your water.
Your cleansing, refreshing, life-giving water.
Amen.

CHAPTER FOUR

Confirmation—Moving toward Christian Adulthood

Being a baby was so natural . . . being a mother was sometimes hard.

They both heard the baby about the same time. And they both hesitated, anxious to see if the other would get up with her. Finally, when he didn't move, Sarah rolled over and flopped the covers back. In the end, responding to the baby's cry always seemed to be her responsibility. Sometimes this made her mad, because even though the baby was nursing, the baby would take a bottle too!

She picked up the tiny bundle of warmth from the middle of the big crib and nuzzled her. The baby quickly responded by searching for her mother's nipple—on her neck! And this tickled the young mother. Being a baby was so natural . . . being a mother was sometimes hard. And it involved decisions . . . like . . . "Do I lie here in the hope that he'll get up?"

But now, all decisions blurred, and her life at this moment was just taking care of this precious little one. She slipped out into the darkened hallway and into the small family room off the kitchen—a good place to nurse the baby because her grandmother's rocker was there.

The rocker nurtured both of them: the child as she was held, nursed, and rocked, and the grown-up child as she enjoyed the rhythms—her child's sucking, swallowing, and breathing, and the loving sway of the old oaken family heirloom.

As they enjoyed their simple ritual, she suddenly became aware of Bill standing in the doorway. The look on his face swept her away to familiar spaces they shared, and she smiled and said, "Hi! What are you doing up?"

"I lay there thinking about you rocking and feeding the baby. I could picture the scene in my head . . . and I wanted to check it out and see if I was right," he answered.

"Well? Were you?" she inquired.

"Yeah. I was. And I wouldn't want to miss it," the young father said as he bent to kiss his beloved.

> *"Although Confirmation is sometimes called the 'sacrament of Christian maturity,' we must not confuse adult faith with the adult age of natural growth, nor forget that the baptismal grace . . . does not need 'ratification' to become effective."*
>
> CCC, 1308

When I was a child, my speech, feelings, and thinking were all those of a child; now that I am an adult, I have no more use for childish ways. What we see now is like a dim image in a mirror; then we shall see face-to-face. What I know now is only partial; then it will be complete—as complete as God's knowledge of me.

Meanwhile these three remain: faith, hope, and love; and the greatest of these is love.

1 Corinthians 13:11–13

The young person must accept the adulthood sought . . .

Change happens. For parents, changing lives for the first child is a huge adjustment. And then raising a child is one adjustment after another! However, for most of us, parenthood usually makes adulthood happen real fast. At least the invitation to mature is there!

But change is hard. For some reason we fight it. Change is one thing if we are the one changing, but it's another thing if it involves our children and the stages they go through! In this case we seem to fight change even more! The interesting thing is that a child is on automatic pilot—growing! We're the ones who must change on purpose! We have to try to stay a little ahead of each stage the child is automatically going through.

And it's hard sometimes! The changes of our lives probably challenge us more than anything we face— especially if it involves children.

As our children grow, we must change house rules, and then change them again. We keep trying to maintain some balance, some semblance of routine. But things keep changing! This may be normal, but those of us who are parents live on the edge of all hell breaking loose!

Moreover, we spend about twenty years (per child!) getting through these changes. Then, just as we see safe land in sight, an interesting dynamic enters the whole process. The young person in our life has to accept the adulthood sought for umpteen years! Another rite of passage is in order.

⚜

Our children are adults on the one hand, still children on the other.

⚜

For teenagers, the stages include events like sixteenth birthdays, the driver's license, the prom, graduation. These events make us feel both happy and sad. But underlying all is our desire to launch our children into the world. That old hunger again! The drive inside us to move them and ourselves forward toward our eventual destination. However, that certainly does not mean it is easy. Strange thoughts enter our mind: "It's time to really grow up! Get with the program! Thirty is just around the corner, and the rest of life is beyond that. There's living to do, and it's time to carry your own weight." The message we deliver to our children can even be so brazen and bold as to sound like "Get a job!"

This launching out into the "real" world used to happen between seventeen or twenty—when a young person married and left home (really left!). Now it's happening even later, because the average age for marriage is around twenty-seven.

Marriage used to mean the time had come to "settle down" (read: "grow up!"). Now, however, some young adults in their early twenties just continue late adolescence. This is both good and bad: Good because marriage specialists and developmental psychologists stress that when people marry at a more mature age, they are better prepared for the married life. Bad because this fact also often means that we parents continue to support young people who are returning or not leaving home and who are unable or unwilling to support themselves! Our children are adults on the one hand, still children on the other.

Saint Paul wrote the above Scripture to a community in dire straits. These early Christians probably had some of the same problems we parents have when we try to move our children into adulthood. Resistance and rebellion!

Paul told the community in Corinth, as he tells us, that we must pass into adulthood, but becoming adult is not enough. We must do more. All our life is a journey; times of passage will

> *In this "God moment," which the husband shares with his wife and with their child, he discovers the holiness of growing up before God.*

continue; and we must accept that we will always be changing, striving, struggling, searching, and changing. Only when we meet our God face-to-face and know God fully will we know completeness, will we know the wholeness and holiness of eternal maturity.

Experiencing those moments of movement toward maturity (as evidenced in the story opening this chapter) is both refreshing and important. One of the most interesting aspects of this process, however, is that as we move through these experiences we don't often recognize them as moments of growth. It is only afterward that the experience can be seen as growth-filled. For example, the young father, perhaps a bit guilty at not getting up with his hungry child himself, does indeed demonstrate care and concern and a new place in his journey when he joins his nursing family. For whatever reason, within him came the invitation— the "message" to grow a little more. To get up out of his warm bed, enter the holiness of his family's moment of family love—and to enjoy the gift of it. And he responded to the invitation. In this "God moment," which the husband shares with his wife and with their child, he discovers the holiness of growing up before God.

". . . catechesis for Confirmation should strive to awaken a sense of belonging to the Church of Jesus Christ, the universal Church, as well as the parish community."

CCC, 1309

🄰
Something has happened to us from within . . .
🄰

If we really knew what we sought from the Church when we asked for the sacrament of Confirmation, someone would probably have to drag us to the church, kicking and screaming all the way. Why? Because when we seek to be confirmed, we should be in somewhat the same fearful state as were the disciples of Jesus when they hid behind locked doors after his ascension.

While momentarily protected and safe, the followers of Jesus knew they couldn't remain in the upper room forever. Yet they were unsure about the crowd outside. Just a few weeks earlier that crowd had called for the crucifixion of Jesus. The disciples weren't exactly sure that they wanted to follow in their leader's footsteps!

We know the rest of the story. They eventually did open the doors and confront the crowd. God's Spirit "fired" them up; they began to move out and into life! To take what Jesus taught and to live it! To be courageous and bold! They grew up! They had followed long enough. Now the Spirit wanted them to lead, to begin the revolution!

The confirming of our faith

Confirmation makes us aware that our faith will make demands on us. But at the same time, the Spirit strengthens us. This is somewhat like exercising: The process of working our muscles weakens us. Still exercising makes our muscles stronger; we become energized.

After Pentecost (when the Holy Spirit filled the disciples with faith and zeal), the disciples of Jesus wondered if they had the courage and strength to do all Jesus had invited them to do. The future probably seemed momentous. Maybe almost impossible. Their doubts about their own abilities probably differed little from ours when we face a major crisis: A loved one dies; an unexpected divorce happens; a doctor diagnoses a child as being incurably ill; we have to put a parent in a nursing home.

What is our first response in situations like these? Often we confess weakness, a feeling that we have reached the end of our rope. We say to ourselves and others, "I don't think I can survive this. I can't go on." We're not just saying something to be saying something; we really mean what we say. The future appears to be an insurmountable wall; we feel that we simply can't do what we have to do.

> *It's the difference between being a totally dependent child and one moving toward adulthood.*

Then comes the second reflection or reaction or response. We think about other people we know who have gone through similar difficulties. They have survived; some might say that the crisis made them stronger. So we go deep within ourselves. And we find ourselves beginning to hope. "Perhaps I can make it." And we begin again to live victory rather than defeat.

At baptism especially if we are infants we say, in a sense, our first yes through others to all life offers. But we ourselves say a stronger yes at our confirmation. What's the difference? It's the difference between being a totally dependent child and one moving toward adulthood.

But the change is more than a physical one of our body growing up. Something has happened to us from within. Something "clicks" and we realize that we are leaving early childhood and entering a whole new, uncharted area for ourselves. Life seems scary and exciting at the same time. But we know that we must move ahead. And again, with that first step, we accept both freedom and responsibility. We begin our Christian adulthood.

Witnessing to the Gospel

At the beginning of Christianity, the early Christians walked a dangerous route, but they knew that moving ahead was absolutely necessary. Eventually God invited

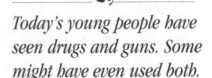

Today's young people have seen drugs and guns. Some might have even used both.

many of these Christians to shed their blood for Jesus. Just as many of his followers are doing today.

The word the Church first used to describe those who literally gave their life as Christians was *martyr,* or *witness.* A witness is one who testifies in public on behalf of another person. (We still use that same language in our courts.) A Christian witness is one who publicly lives the kind of life Jesus lived. This life is both demanding and rewarding. (Rewarding, that is, if you have a broad definition of reward!) As we witness with the love that Jesus showed us, we may even wake up in the middle of the night to care for a hungry baby or to care for a very unhungry spouse.

Confirmation is a sacrament in which we respond to the Gospel's invitation to convert our heart and change our life. Let's picture a group of young people being confirmed. First, they gather in the church. They may have spent more than a year talking about the demands and challenges of their faith. They know (some more than others) that confirmation is serious business.

By now they realize that much of what's in their world, their school, their entertainment, their social life is not really compatible with Christian values. They struggle to be accepted by their friends while remaining their own persons. They want to have the freedom to go along or resist, to say yes or no, and to be decisive about both.

What's happening in their lives can pull these young people apart. They hear their parents talking about what life was like for them when they were young. The parents laugh over stories about family squabbles and kids trying to sneak a smoke on the side; they reminiscence about days of peace and tranquility. Today's youth have seen drugs and guns. Some might have even used both. These are different times—hard times.

The primary symbol of confirmation is the anointing with oil by the bishop as he lays his hand on the head of the person being confirmed. This anointing consecrates (blesses) in a special way those being confirmed. They are made holy. In what sense do we mean this? Not in the sense of being separated from the world, but in the sense of being a sacred presence in our universe.

These newly confirmed young people become Christians in and to the world. They may become like the leaven or yeast in the dough that will become the sustaining loaf of bread. We may not directly see the leaven at all because it works in secret, quietly. The loaf of bread totally absorbs it. But we know that the yeast is within the dough because we can see how the bread grows and expands. Change takes place deep within the substance of the dough.

What other symbols can we use for the newly confirmed? They may become like "a city on a mountain" or "a lamp on a stand" (as the Gospel says). They may stand out as those who are different from the crowd. They may carry a different set of values. Values that can make the world holy and whole.

Fuller membership in the Church

Usually a bishop administers the sacrament of Confirmation. (Sometimes the bishop will give permission for a priest to do so in his place, but the symbolic meaning of confirmation remains as part of the ministry of the bishop.) This implies that the confirmed person is being brought into a deeper, more active and involved relationship with the Church community. One is moving to a more adult identity and role.

For the one being confirmed, the realm of freedom grows as does the burden of responsibility. The views of the confirmed become more important for the life of the Church. In fact, some parishes allow confirmed youth to serve on special parish committees. They have both a right and a responsibility to speak.

Someone else can drive to the convenience store at midnight to get bread and milk!

And the rest of the parish has a responsibility to listen.

This pattern is very common in families. Earlier we used the example of receiving a license to drive a car. We know that cars are very important in contemporary life. They bring us freedom of movement, but they are also a major expense on the family budget. Cars can be dangerous too; automobile accidents take away far too many young lives.

Having a new driver in the family alters the dynamics of life. Sometimes it's a major shift; sometimes this passage is helpful for families because someone other than the parent can become the all-purpose chauffeur for the younger children. Someone else can drive to the convenience store to get bread and milk!

Most families, however, also know the other side of the story. A shortage of family cars quickly becomes obvious. We begin to worry about the new driver, to imagine the worst. Cars can bring teens to places of action, yet the action may be neither lawful nor safe.

Once again, the two-sided reality of freedom and responsibility surfaces. But that's good. That's the way God made us. Freedom is one of the greatest gifts God has given us. Yes, there is risk, but God intends to create newness in the world. And the move from old to new, the experience of change is all part of the world as wonderfully made by God.

God knew exactly what was needed to get the followers of Jesus going, to fire them up!

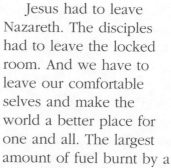

Jesus had to leave Nazareth. The disciples had to leave the locked room. And we have to leave our comfortable selves and make the world a better place for one and all. The largest amount of fuel burnt by a rocket upon takeoff is spent in the first second of the mission. That's because it takes so much energy to move from "just sitting there" to flight.

Getting in touch with the grace or energy from confirmation is like that. Perhaps that's one reason why the Spirit came to those first, fearful disciples in the form of fire. Fire is as much a symbol of energy as we can imagine. God knew exactly what was needed to get the followers of Jesus going, to get them outside, to launch them into the world, to fire them up!

And with our own confirmation, Pentecost (the coming of the Holy Spirit) is still happening. God still desires to move us out of our laziness, our fears, our doubts. Certainly something quite powerful launched Bill, the young man in our opening story, off his comfortable bed and out to the side of his nursing wife.

*Confirmation challenges us
to confirm our faith . . .
in ordinary events . . .*

The history of the sacrament of Confirmation is proof that we belong to a living, growing, learning Church. The Church first connected this sacrament with baptism, then with children of grade-school age, then high school and young adulthood, and then back again to baptism. And the movement continues, because fully understanding confirmation and its significance and placement in our lives continues. Today the church is reaffirming the ancient practice of offering the sacraments of Baptism, Confirmation and Eucharist in that order. This emphasizes that participation in the Eucharist is the pinnacle experience for Christians. While the practice varies from diocese to diocese, some fairly young children will now be receiving Confirmation. Still, the sacrament continues to signify movement toward adulthood.

The way we as a Church community keep determining what confirmation means in our lives is in itself a gift. For this sacrament challenges and invites us to continue to understand God better, particularly God the Holy Spirit. Just when we think we have grasped a new understanding, it seems to gently slip away and we must work harder to find new ways to understand more.

Maybe this is true because confirming—living—our faith is so much a part of being a child of God that as humans we don't have the means to understand it yet. Nonetheless, the process is good for us, for it helps us clarify our own faith. It brings to the front the need to ask ourselves every day, "Am I firm in my faith?"

In fact, God invites us to ask and answer this question hundreds of times every day. When do we ask the question? In all the big and little moments of our lives. Confirmation challenges us to confirm our faith as we witness to our faith each and every day in the ordinary events of our life.

For example, we witness when we get up to celebrate the Eucharist on Sunday and other adults do not. We witness through a quiet, gentle living of our faith, no matter what. When yet another child asks something of our tired bodies, we can be open to the needs of another and respond or we can close ourselves to love and react in anger or rejection. We can say yes again and yet again. Yes to loving the way Jesus did. And each time we do this, we confirm our faith.

Confirmation invites and challenges us in big ways too—through the moments of our lives that perhaps challenge our faith the most. Times when we get angry at God! For instance, a time when death looms over the family, and we just want God to change everything!

Yet we confirm our faith as we accept, and perhaps even embrace, God's will by caring for the person until death comes. We love him or her to the end and beyond. And perhaps we share our faith with this loved one by discussing death and our belief in a life ever-lasting. Perhaps, together, we and the person who is dying celebrate his or her life. And together we confirm our faith in God's promise of new life.

We face other big challenges—like when a divorce happens. Then we need to find comfort in those around us, and recognize our God in them. And even in our pain, we ritualize this part of our journey through the legal system and the need to let go and go on. And our God is with us in a million ways, even in the middle of the night. We confirm our faith when we accept these— life's hardest challenges—and in a thousand ways say "Yes, Lord."

And we confirm our faith in our hope for a better tomorrow; we confirm our faith when we work to make the world a better place for others. We confirm our faith when we care about the environment, about our brothers and sisters across the street and across the world, and about the precious persons with whom we live and work and play and pray. (That's what our young father did when he got up out of his warm bed to be with his nursing family.)

Look back over your day. Have you experienced such a *con-firming* moment today? Have you had a moment when you could have closed yourself to the needs of those who look to you for love, when you could have turned away but you didn't? Have you tuned into the pain, the request, the challenge? Have you loved as Jesus loved? Have you accepted the invitation to grow and change and to say, "Yes, God!" If that hasn't happened today, then perhaps you'll have another opportunity when you finish reading this.

> " 'Now when the apostles at Jerusalem heard that Samaria had received the word of God, they sent to them Peter and John, who came down and prayed for them. . . . Then they laid their hands on them and they received the Holy Spirit.' " (Acts 8:14–17)
>
> CCC, 1315

A Psalm

The Lord is my shepherd;
I have everything I need.
He lets me rest in fields of green grass
and leads me to quiet pools of fresh water.
He gives me new strength.
He guides me in the right paths, as he has promised.
Even if I go through the deepest darkness,
I will not be afraid, Lord, for you are with me.
Your shepherd's rod and staff protect me.

Psalm 23:1–4

On Those Days, Lord Jesus

On those days, Lord Jesus,
When I miss my kids and grandkids,
When I listen for the sound of just another
	human voice,
When I seem only to have memories to live by,
When I long for the phone to ring,
When I'm glad even to get junk mail,
When everyone seems to have someone but me,
When I am afraid to go to bed at night,
When I feel, oh, so lonely,
(again)
Lord Jesus, give me the strength
To make it.
No! To live again!
With a twinkle in my eye
And a fire in my heart
Remind me that you are with me,
And with you and me together anything—
	and everything—is possible.
In fact, I have a feeling that
You understand this more than I do.
You are that kind of God.
Amen.

CHAPTER FIVE

Eucharist—Our Sacred Family Meal

. . . asking God to bless Brad's grandpa and their pizza too . . .

"Please, please, please, Mom?" her twelve-year-old begged. "Brad's mom said he could! And we could get a video, and we'll go right to sleep, I promise! Please?"

It was Friday afternoon, and she was dead tired. She was looking forward to just getting home after work and crashing. The thought of taking care of another twelve-year-old boy in addition to her other two kids was stressful. But love for Sean won out.

"Okay," she said. "But you need to do your chores anyway, remember? And I think it's your night for dishes."

"I will. Thanks, Mom. See ya," he replied.

The last hour of work was worse than the first seven. By the time she unlocked the car, rain was pouring down and traffic was already backing up. "Darn it!" she thought. "There's no way I'll be able to cook tonight. I'll just have to squeeze money for a pizza again. Darn."

Three thousand other parents were doing the same. So by the time she got the pizza and stopped to get bread and toilet paper, it was later still. "The kids will be off the wall," she thought. "I'm sorry Brad is coming over. This isn't a good night."

The house was relatively quiet, which both surprised and concerned her. But they were all in safe places. Brad was already in Sean's room when she opened her son's bedroom door.

"Hi, guys," she greeted them, and then saw that Sean's look wasn't his usual joyful face. When she glanced at Brad, she realized he'd been crying.

"What's the matter, Honey?" she asked him.

Sean answered for his friend. "Mom, Brad's grandpa died. And he wanted to come over here to get away from the sad house. He didn't tell me until he got here."

Her heart melted for the child. She knew how close he was to his grandpa. He talked about him all the time. And she was touched that he wanted to come here, to her hectic house. "I'm so sorry, Brad. Was he sick?"

"No. He just died sleeping. My mom said it would be good to come over here. But I don't have to eat here. I had a sandwich," he hastened to assure her.

"Of course you'll eat here, Brad. Unless, of course, you don't like pizza with everything but mushrooms and onions—just good ol' cheese and pepperoni, like we always have!" she teased.

"Wow! I love that kind! I didn't know you were having pizza! Yum! Thanks a lot."

She quickly reheated the pizza. Soon the whole family was gathered around the table. Everyone was quiet, because none of the kids knew what, if anything, to say to Brad about his grandfather.

So she broke the silence and suggested they say a simple prayer, asking God to bless Brad's grandpa and to bless their pizza too. The prayer bridged the silence into bedlam as the children grabbed pizza from the middle of the table. "Amen," she said to herself. So be it. Life goes on.

After this, Jesus went across Lake Galilee (or, Lake Tiberias, as it is also called). A large crowd followed him, because they had seen his miracles of healing the sick. Jesus went up a hill and sat down with his disciples. The time for Passover Festival was near. Jesus looked around and saw that a large crowd was coming to him, so he asked Philip, "Where can we buy enough food to feed all these people?" (He said this to test Philip; actually he already knew what he would do.)

Philip answered, "For everyone to have even a little, it would take more than two hundred silver coins to buy enough bread."

Another one of his disciples, Andrew, who was Simon Peter's brother, said, "There is a boy here who has five loaves of barley bread and two fish. But they will certainly not be enough for all these people."

"Make the people sit down," Jesus told them. (There was a lot of grass there.) So all the people sat down; there were about five thousand men. Jesus took the bread, gave thanks to God, and distributed it to the people who were sitting there. He did the same with the fish, and they all had as much as they wanted. When they were all full, he said to his disciples, "Gather the pieces left over; let us not waste a bit." So they gathered them all and filled twelve baskets with the pieces left over from the five barley loaves which the people had eaten.

Seeing this miracle that Jesus had performed, the people there said, "Surely this is the Prophet who was to come into the world!" Jesus knew that they were about to come and seize him in order to make him king by force; so he went off again to the hills by himself.

John 6:1–14

What a scene! A sea of people have come to hear Jesus speak and to learn from him. Obviously, only one of them, a child, planned for the fact that the day might be long—and there wouldn't be any hot dog stands!

Jesus responds by feeding five thousand with . . . a child's lunch box!

And because Jesus is such a caring, loving person, he feels obliged to feed the people. No. He *wants* to feed them! After all, they're hungry, and when people are hungry, we feed them!

And the scene continues, for Jesus responds to the hunger of the milling crowd by feeding five thousand with the contents of a child's lunch box! Jesus was always feeding—both the body and the spirit.

"Well, just feed them!" he says to his followers. "This is what you do, guys, feed the multitudes! Now and forever more! Feed their spirits, feed their bodies. Bring them to me. Break bread and distribute it . . . in memory of me. Recognize me in the breaking of the bread . . . now and forever! Do this for the least . . . then you do it for me."

Sharing pizza isn't often seen as a holy meal. However, in our opening story, the mother and her oldest child were greatly concerned about their young friend. The family gathered to break the "bread," yes, but also to be with their guest, who was hurting. And prayer happened, thanksgiving to God for not only the pizza, but for the fact that we are a hopeful people and that life goes on.

With all these realities, Jesus was indeed with them—just as he was remembered in the breaking of the bread.

_____ ✌ _____

Deep understanding of anything often begins with the attitude of wonder.

_____ ✌ _____

If frosting goes with cake, so does the Mass go with Catholicism. The official documents of the Church call the Mass the source and the summit of the Christian life.

While we don't know everything that happened in the early Church, we do know that when people met together, they usually did so to "break bread," which meant they were remembering what Jesus did and what Jesus told them to do in his memory.

The Gospels also tell us that when Jesus appeared to his followers after the resurrection, he often came at mealtime. And that's why the Eucharist is so important. It is the primary way Catholics connect with Jesus. We connect in the breaking of the bread.

The Eucharist is not just one of seven sacraments, but rather, it is the one from which the other six draw their meaning. (Baptism and confirmation prepare us for full participation in the Eucharist.)

Food for the journey
Deep understanding of anything often begins with the attitude of wonder. A good "wondering" clears the mind of earlier understandings that may fall short of a fuller insight. Many Catholics have been learning about the Mass and the Eucharist for their whole lifetime. Right from the first time they accompanied their family to church and asked in their own way, "What's going on here? Why do I have to keep quiet?"

The first thing to notice about the celebration of the Eucharist is that in the beginning it was simple. Early Jewish converts, especially those who were part of the liturgy and ceremonies of the Temple itself, probably felt disappointed when they realized that this "new religion" was plain and unadorned.

"Where are all the rituals? The elaborate furniture? The robes? The high altar? The slaughtering of animals? The blood and so forth?" they must have asked. "You mean we're replacing all that with breaking bread around an ordinary table? Hasn't something been lost? You call this an improvement?"

True, the celebration of the Eucharist was ordinary and commonplace. At least on the surface. In fact, it couldn't be more so. People had to eat every day, and bread was about as basic a food as anyone could imagine. The same could be said about the wine. Again, common fare.

The early followers of Jesus created the liturgy of the early Church as a direct response to the words and example of Jesus. (Liturgy manifests the way we celebrate—the words and the actions and the simple materials of our world that we use.) Jesus had come to reveal something very simple, yet totally profound: God is present in the ordinary—in the food and in the people who share this food. And Jesus, too, is there. The early believers recognized him, the Gospels say, in the breaking of the bread.

God is present in the ordinary—in the food and in the people who share this food.

When Jesus walked the dusty roads of Palestine, he often talked about wheat. He described the natural process by which the seed, planted in good soil, dies, breaks open, is transformed, and then grows into the waving stalk of wheat.

The farmer harvests the wheat and grinds it into flour. The cook mixes the flour with water and yeast and bakes the dough. Then the family gathers. Someone serves the bread and the members around the table share it.

This process goes back as far as anyone can remember. Everyone in Jesus' time was familiar with these matters. Yet, Jesus used this process to help his listeners explore the mystery of God's presence.

Bread has sustained life in civilizations that were already ancient when Jesus was born. Jesus took this foundational symbolism and transformed it. In his teachings—his words and actions—he brought wheat and yeast and bread under the power of God's love. He blessed the bread, broke it, and gave it to those gathered to celebrate in his name. Through the power of God, Jesus changed bread into his body, his real body (which was broken on the cross). He then gave this body for his followers.

The symbol is brilliant, yet so simple. Still, all the meaning is there. God sustains life and nourishes us in that which is so common, so ordinary—table bread. Our God is a God of the ordinary. Sometimes we forget this. Sometimes we place God apart from that which is immediate to us. But God, like a family tradition or a battered and beat-up wonderful old kitchen table, wants to be part of our everyday life.

The sacrificial meal of the Mass

From its initial, very simple beginnings, the rite of the Mass has evolved over the centuries. As most Catholics know, the Church has recently gone through a period of intense study of its history.

Our God is a God of the ordinary. Sometimes we forget this.

Driven by a vision of the Mass articulated at Vatican II, the Church has renewed the rituals of the Mass with the intent of making them more accessible to all of us. To do this the Church has made a number of changes: (1) The Church changed the language of the Mass from

Latin (which, of course, was not the original language of the Mass) to the vernacular language of the people, the local language. Throughout the world, people celebrate the Mass in their own language. (2) The Church also simplified the symbolic gestures of the Mass and removed repetition.. (3) Next, the Church divided the various roles in the Mass among the faithful (those committed to the Catholic tradition).

The important point of these changes is to bring the Mass closer to us, because the Church wants the Mass to be the sacramental celebration of the whole community of believers.

Two *central ideas* form the core of our understanding of the Mass: (1) The Mass re-presents the central events of our faith: the death and resurrection of Jesus. While Jesus died and was raised from death only once, the Mass brings the effects of these saving actions into the presence of the assembled Christian community. (2) The Mass gives us the opportunity to connect our life, with all its joys and sufferings, with Christ Jesus' offering of his life for us. And we do this right now. The Mass places us, so to speak, in an immediate relationship with Jesus and with the power that comes from encountering him in the midst of our own life.

> *Slowly we—the Church—are beginning to understand.*

Jesus comes to us in the breaking of the bread, the Eucharist. In the act of receiving the host and sharing the wine, we welcome the person of Jesus into ourselves as food or nourishment for our own Christian life. Jesus comes to dwell with us, and we join ourselves to him. This is union in as full a sense as we can imagine. We are made part of the Body of Christ, just as Jesus, food for the journey, becomes part of our body.

But there is more. In receiving Christ Jesus, we also receive the whole Christ—his Body, the Church. We not only unite with Jesus but also with others. The Mass is a shared meal. Slowly we—the Church—are beginning to understand and appreciate this rich and essential social aspect of our celebration.

To symbolize this communal dimension of the Mass, the Church has restored the beautiful ritual of exchanging peace. One of the earliest accounts of the Mass (from about 150 years after the birth of Christ) mentions this deeply meaningful gesture.

> *With the invention of the bread slicer, we even forget the simple gesture of "breaking" bread.*

Through and in the Eucharist, we connect, or join, not only with Jesus but also with all those who believe in Christ Jesus and the God he proclaimed. We affirm our belief that we are one body in Christ. The exchange of peace symbolizes this oneness.

When we participate in the Eucharist, we participate in a sacrificial meal. Consider how the creation of a typical family meal has a profound sense of sacrifice associated with it. Farmers toil greatly to grow our food; we labor long hours to earn the money to buy the food; then we work to prepare the food for our family to eat. In a sense, the sweat and sacrifice of many people make our eating possible.

One of the losses of an affluent society with a developed technology is that we take things for granted. We lose touch with nature and with natural activities. We lose an awareness of the rich natural symbolism of human life. With the invention of the bread slicer, we even forget the simple gesture of "breaking" bread.

All this technology makes entering the world of natural symbolism more difficult for us. This is one of the reasons why the sacraments of the Church may no longer excite our imagination or make an impression on our consciousness. Water, oil, bread, and wine are basic. But we can lose a sense of basics when everything we see and touch is fabricated, wrapped in plastic, or ordered at a counter.

The sharing of food is the sharing of life. The work of many hands has brought the meal to the table.

> *Good wine adds something special to a meal and to a gathering.*

Satisfying our hunger is a basic human need, but hunger has many meanings. We hunger not just for food, but also for companionship. In fact, the word *companion* has a wonderful meaning. It comes from the Latin *panis,* meaning "bread" and the Latin *com* or *cum*, meaning "with." A companion is one with whom we share bread.

And the Eucharist is a shared meal. This sacrament joins the most common human need—our need for food—with our need for God. And God responds by feeding us the bread of life, the bread made into the body of the Lord Jesus. This bread is food for our soul.

The symbolism of the wine is important too. Wine made into the blood of Christ goes back to the New Testament and its stories about our covenant relationship with God. Ancient people sealed covenants, or agreements, with blood. The many sacrifices of the Temple were covenant sacrifices. These rituals expressed the Jews' special relationship with God.

From a Christian perspective, the shedding of the blood of Jesus established the *new covenant*, the new relationship between God and us. This new covenant joins us to the ultimate source of all life—the God of life and love.

Wine brings about special feelings within those who drink it. It can bring a sense of lightness, of enjoyment, of satisfaction. Good wine adds something special to a meal and to a gathering. At the Last Supper, Jesus shared wine with his disciples. Today, the wine used at Mass helps us remember God's special generosity in giving us the fruit of the vine and the work of human hands.

Jesus tells us at each Eucharist to take and eat his body, which he has given for us and to drink his blood of the new covenant, which he has shed for us and for many, for the forgiveness of sins. He asks us to perform these actions in memory of him.

Word and sacrament

The Mass, sometimes now called the eucharistic liturgy, is divided into two parts: the Liturgy of the Word and the Liturgy of the Eucharist. Again, we can trace this pattern to the earliest accounts of the

> *Both testaments, however, are part of our faith history; they are like our own family's story.*

Mass. The first part of the Mass brings to us the Word of God, which is from Scripture—the Bible. We listen to God addressing us in the present moment.

The readings for the Liturgy of the Word come from both the Old Testament (before Jesus' birth) and the New Testament (after Jesus' birth). Both testaments, however, are part of our faith history; they are like our own family's story. With these two testaments, we go back to the very beginnings of our faith story.

Vatican II (a series of meetings in the Church during the early sixties) recommended that sermons, or homilies, connect the Scripture readings to the life of those assembled in the church. The reforms of Vatican II emphasized the importance of Scripture in the life of Catholics. For many, this was new. Why? Before Vatican II, Catholics seemed to emphasize the sacraments in the worship, while Protestants focused on the Scriptures.

Today, Catholics have reclaimed the importance of the Bible. This return of Catholics to the Bible has been a gradual but welcome change. Catholics now read, study, and discuss the Bible with a new enthusiasm. Catholics also share the Bible with others in interfaith (more than one religion) families. All these changes represent a positive movement toward the oneness for which Jesus prayed.

The second part of the Mass, the Liturgy of the Eucharist, involves three basic actions: (1) The community brings the gifts of bread and wine to the altar. These gifts represent our lives. (2) The priest accepts these gifts in the name of God and repeats the words of Jesus. God then changes these gifts of bread and wine into the body and blood of Jesus. (Our tradition calls this *transubstantiation,* a word meaning that the substance of the bread and the wine are truly changed into the substance of the body and blood of Jesus.) This change of our gifts into the gift of Jesus re-presents the sacrifice of Jesus, who freely chose to give up his life for our sins and for the sins of the world. (3) Jesus comes to us as food and drink, as nourishment for our spiritual journey. Jesus comes to us and we come to Jesus. In this action, Jesus unites us with God.

The Mass, the Eucharistic banquet, is our great expression of thanksgiving. (In Greek, one of the languages of the early Church, the word *eucharist* means "the giving of thanks.") And all of this is why the Church calls the Mass the source (base) and summit (top) of our Christian life.

✏
Nourishing ourselves and others is vital to being human.

✏

We all know how important food and water are to our existence. Without one or the other, we die. In addition to that, we have made the need to eat and to drink a wonderful part of being human. We have surrounded this basic human need with much creativity and celebration. We don't just eat bread; we have cookies and doughnuts, a variety of cereals and wonderful strawberry shortcake! We don't just drink water; we have beer and soft drinks and lemonade—and now, even flavored water!

We aren't satisfied with just the basic food groups; we have to do them up royally! And besides celebrating in our homes with "Time to eat!" when we gather to share food and share talk, we also have made food a way to honor people or impress people or make ourselves feel better.

We go to fancy and unfancy places to eat food that somebody else cooks! And, unless we have to, we rarely go alone. We like to visit restaurants only with others.

Let us not forget that there are groups of peoples in some countries who sit around their huts and campfires to share their food and never visit a restaurant. Still, the sharing of food, the breaking of bread is a vital shared aspect of these communities. The symbolism of sharing food pervades all humankind. Nourishing ourselves and others is vital to being human. Still others have no food. Our media brings this reality to our supper tables.

Naturally, then, Jesus used the symbol of food to teach us about living in community and about caring for ourselves, for one another, and for God. In the breaking of the bread, Jesus nourishes us. And by sharing in this food, by taking and eating it, by saying "Amen" when we hear "the Body of Christ," we are saying "Yes, I believe. Yes, I share in Christ's life. Yes, I am part of Christ and God's family. Yes, I share in the Body of Christ, that body that contains all the others. Yes, I belong to and am part of all."

As we each stand up with others and move forward to receive the Eucharist from a member of the community who awaits us, we are taking new steps in our journey. Each time we perform these actions, the moment is new, and again we are saying to ourselves, to those around us, and to Jesus, "Here I am, Jesus." And Jesus answers, "And here, too, am I."

Then together, as a community nourished for our journey, we depart the assembly; we get in our car or we walk home. And to all we meet—family, friends, colleagues at work, neighbors, those at the grocery store or in the park—we bring the God who has nourished us, who has become one with us, who is forming us into holy and whole persons. Our God is a part of us, and we belong to God and to all others. We become food for others

Sustained by love, we make it through another day.

Next time you take part in Mass, watch the wonderful mix of people who joined you that day. Getting to the church may not have been easy—what with crawling out of bed and perhaps dressing children and getting the show on the road! But those who come, come to join with you in what we celebrate and believe. Be aware of the mix of ages, of clothing, of gestures, of the faces of those who believe with you and walk with you to receive the Eucharist.

And then, when you return home, see the same wonderful mix of people who gather to break bread in your own home or other holy places. Like the family sharing pizza in our opening story, see and feel our God in those who gather around the table or even on the floor of the family room. See these people, these loved ones, as gathered to celebrate belonging to one another—in and through and with Christ Jesus.

And finally know and embrace the holiness of both the Mass and the home experience.

"The Lord, having loved those who were his own, loved them to the end. Knowing that the hour had come . . . in the course of a meal he washed their feet and gave them the commandment of love."

CCC, 1337

A Psalm

From the sky you send rain on the hills,
    and the earth is filled with your blessings.
You make grass grow for the cattle
    and plants for us to use,
so that we can grow our crops
    and produce wine to make us happy,
    olive oil to make us cheerful,
    and bread to give us strength.

Psalm 104:13–15

Bless Us Again, Dear God

Today I thank you, dear God,
For sometime today I will eat.
At least I live in the hopes and promise
    of that.
But I never really know
Until I actually have the food in front of me
Or find it in the cupboard or fridge,
Or scrape up enough money to buy
Something good, and solid, and nourishing,
Or hope to find a place of caring and concern
To give me nourishment for my body, mind, and spirit.

Yet
I never really know for sure each day, dear God.
I just live in faith
That the food I find in my kitchen
Or in others'
Will fulfill your promise
To be with me always.
In the breaking of the bread.
Amen.

CHAPTER SIX

Penance/Reconciliation— Welcome Back Home

It started with his eyes . . . it was the look of forgiveness.

She didn't know if she could do it. Her life was so different since she left. And it wasn't only the time that had passed; *she* was different. And she guessed he was too.

At least that's what the kids had said.

"You won't know Dad," young Donald had said. "He's really different now."

But for some reason, she just moved forward with the plan to meet with him, almost as if she were on automatic pilot. She still felt fear and reluctance, but she continued making all the plans and doing all she needed to do to get to the counselor's office.

And now the time had come to leave.

She looked at herself in the mirror and found herself checking her appearance, wondering if he'd like the way she looked. He used to. Suddenly she found herself self-conscious. "Geez, I'm really getting paranoid. I want him to like me again. Love me again! I'm really concerned about how I look! This is important to me!"

The counselor's office was across town, and she had more time to get nervous and to worry. She also had more time to think.

Her thoughts ran wild. "What if he says, 'No way! After what you did . . . forget it!' But he wouldn't be coming to meet me if that were true." She had to believe he wanted her in his life again. In their lives again.

Then she was at the office building. She recognized his van in the parking lot next to the skyscraper. He was already there. "God, I'm so scared," she said out loud. She took the elevator up to the fifth floor. When the elevator door opened, he was there. Waiting.

A surge of "He looks older" swept over her and quickly became "He looks so good."

Their eyes locked and both their mouths trembled into tentative smiles.

Then it happened. It started with his eyes and then his mouth. It was the look of forgiveness she knew so well.

That was all it took. Her whole being felt a wave of weightlessness. Together, they turned toward the counselor's office to begin.

"Jesus not only forgave sins, . . . he reintegrated forgiven sinners into the community of the People of God. . . . A remarkable sign of this . . . Jesus receives sinners at his table. . . ."

CCC, 1443

This was how the birth of Jesus Christ took place.
His mother Mary was engaged to Joseph, but before
they were married, she found out that she was
going to have a baby by the Holy Spirit. Joseph was
a man who always did what was right, but he did
not want to disgrace Mary publicly; so he made
plans to break the engagement privately. While he
was thinking about this, an angel of the Lord
appeared to him in a dream and said, "Joseph,
descendant of David, do not be afraid to take Mary
to be your wife. . . ."

Now all this happened in order to make come
true what the Lord had said through the prophet . . .
So when Joseph woke up, he married Mary.

Matthew 1:18–20, 22, 24

*They are ordinary
people . . . with an extraordinary role to play.*

We have heard the story
of Mary and Joseph so
many times we probably
miss the point. At least,
we probably don't fill in
the blanks. Let's imagine
these two people. They
are probably both young and in love. We know they are
betrothed (a commitment, deeper than an engagement,
that takes a form of divorce to cancel). They are
ordinary people like us, with an extraordinary role
to play in life.

Now let's imagine further: The young woman, Mary,
is pregnant, unmarried. She's probably afraid. Maybe
she doesn't understand what's happening. Perhaps she's
terrified that Joseph will abandon her.

Do they argue? Does she leave him standing there
after he tells her he doesn't know what he's going to
do? Does she run back to her mother? Perhaps he meets

with friends to think about everything. Perhaps he's confused, scared, angry, sad.

Perhaps, then, he lies down to sleep and spends the night tossing and turning as we all do when we have a huge problem. When at last he falls asleep, he receives a directive from God. He awakes with his heart changed and his mind made up. He rushes to Mary.

Thoughts race through his mind. "What will she say? Is she still mad?" They experience reconciliation. They touch, kiss, perhaps give each other a long, long hug.

The couple in our opening story could be just like Mary and Joseph. Only they know what happened between them before they came for counseling. What matters is their willingness to make things better. What matters is their hope and faith in tomorrow, possibly together.

Forgiveness is a wonderful reality. Forgiveness doesn't always mean that a couple gets back together, but this can happen nonetheless between any two of us whose relationship is damaged. Sometimes forgiveness starts as a little flicker of letting go of the anger, the hurt, the sadness, the fear. Just a flicker that then gets larger until we experience a warm feeling toward the person again.

Other times forgiveness starts with a decision to forgive; and the actuality of forgiveness, the flicker and eventual forgiveness follow. But forgiveness must start somewhere. For some of us, it begins in the middle of our chest, in the heart area. Right there, where we feel what we call love most of the time. A flicker, sort of like our God whispering. We just barely hear the word, then the reality surrounds us. For some of us it happens in the middle of the night.

Our God works like that. Gently, ever so gently.

⌒

*All humans miss the
mark at some time
or other.*

⌒

The space between people can be sacred. Across that space can flow words of love and gestures of help. The energy or fire of the Holy Spirit can enter that space and make things happen. In the New Testament, we see a gradual unfolding of the meaning that can exist between people when they let their love of God parallel their love of neighbor.

We can't say we love God unless we show that love to our neighbor. If we don't do that, we aren't living in the truth of things. Any vital and genuine Christian spirituality must include full recognition of the importance of "neighborlove."

But the space that goodness could fill can be filled with sin. When the New Testament uses the word *sin,* it has a religious, social, and secular meaning. *Sin* means "missing the mark." It's like shooting an arrow and hitting a tree instead of the target. It's like driving from one place to another and missing an exit.

And who of us has not missed the mark with our neighbors? Who has not hurt others in either word or thought or deed? Who has not overlooked our neighbor's need?

All of us have missed the mark of being a true follower of Jesus; all of us have sinned because we refused to love. All humans miss the mark at some time or other.

Why this discussion of sin? Because we are now talking about the sacrament of Reconciliation, also called Penance. (Some simply refer to this sacrament as "confession.") This sacrament has two primary aspects: our sinfulness and the abundant mercy of God.

From deep within the tradition of the Church comes the practice of bringing God's forgiveness to the sinner. The value of connecting sin with forgiveness is obvious. Burdened with sin (separation from God), we cannot reach the goal of holiness and wholeness that God intends for us. Failing to reach our goal, we would, so to speak, really miss the mark.

But our God is not that kind of God. God loves, as the psalms often say, with an everlasting love. We sin and God pursues us, turns toward us with open arms and a compassionate heart. And as we turn back to God in sorrow, God forgives.

And when God forgives, God holds nothing back. We are brought back into a love relationship with God. Our love for God grows. God embraces us and we know our Creator even better.

The history of Penance

From deep within the tradition of the Church comes the practice of forgiveness.

As Jesus neared the end of his public ministry, he gave his apostles a wonderful task: to make God's forgiveness available to people. During Jesus' own ministry, he went about healing the ailments not only of the body but also of the spirit.

In the name of God, Jesus forgave sin, which keeps the human spirit from wholeness. Jesus gave this same power to the Church. In celebrating the sacrament of Reconciliation, we enter that sacred space of God's guaranteed forgiveness.

In the early Church, Christians rarely used the sacrament of Reconciliation. The Church thought that one could receive the sacrament only once during a lifetime! Also, the Church celebrated the sacrament only in the context of serious sin, like the sin of murder or apostasy (denying the faith).

Apostasy has an interesting history. In the early years, the Roman government often persecuted and killed Christians. The army would arrest and jail everyone who believed in Jesus and in the God he proclaimed. Those strong in their faith willingly presented themselves to the troops. Others, weak in their faith and probably just plain scared, decided that this was a good time to keep quiet.

Like Peter at the time of Jesus' passion, these Christians denied their identity. At some later date, the emperor or local magistrate would call off the persecution or suspend it. Then those who had denied their faith in order to save their necks asked the others to reinstate them in the Christian community. The "youthful" Christians called these Christians *apostates* or *lapsi,* meaning "the fallen ones."

> *Then those who had denied their faith in order to save their necks had second thoughts.*

The community of believers debated what to do. Should they allow the lapsi to be reinstated? This was a burning question.

Because God is a God of forgiveness, they determined they should give the fallen ones a second chance. The process or ritual the Church used in the reinstatement was the sacrament of Penance. The *penance* referred to the way the lapsi had to make up for their denial. Often the Church asked the lapsi to do a form of public service, not unlike that required in secular judicial systems today.

In about the seventh century, after the various peoples of Asia had conquered much of the Christian world, the Church needed to reevangelize Europe.

Irish monks brought not only the heart of the faith (Jesus and the Gospels) but also certain religious practices. One of those practices was the frequent use of the sacrament of Penance. Instead of only receiving penance once during a lifetime, the Irish began to use this sacrament as a way of developing ordinary holiness.

The Irish practice of celebrating penance extended to the whole of one's spiritual life, which included lesser infractions, or venial sins, and not just serious sin. Also, those who forgave in the name of Jesus often gave spiritual advice—an early form of what we call spiritual direction.

Eventually this way of celebrating the sacrament of Penance worked its way into the daily life of Catholics— a pattern developed for the reception of the sacrament still followed today: We reflect on our life, identify those events in which we failed to love, and feel sorrow for offending God and those whom we have sinned against.

The Irish began to use it as a way of developing ordinary holiness.

Then, because the Church embodies in human form the presence and power of God, we come to the Church community in the person of the priest and confess our sin. (Called confession.)

Having heard the confession of the penitent, the priest makes present the forgiveness of God through a symbolic gesture and words. (We need to remember that we are receiving God's forgiveness and not just the priest's.) The priest then gives us a penance, which is usually the recitation of certain prayers or the doing of a good deed. Often, at the end of the celebration, the priest tells us to go in peace, and we embrace once again our positive relationship with God and the Church community, the Body of Christ. The effect of the sacrament is both peace of mind (we know that God has forgiven us) and a commitment to live a more loving life in the future.

Forgiveness and reconnecting with others

In the Our Father, we find the challenging words "Forgive us our trespasses as we forgive those who trespass against us." We ask for forgiveness, but our

We make forgiveness real only when we express it in words and deeds.

prayer includes a commitment from us to forgive others. We may say these words out of routine, but once in a while their power may enter us and cause us to examine our own willingness to forgive.

But to forgive others—with the thoroughness of God's forgiveness of us—that's saying something!

Forgiveness has many dimensions. Forgiving another in our heart is one thing, but we make that forgiveness real only when we express it in words and deeds to the one who has hurt us. Also, to forgive means that we let go of vengeance or getting even. This is hard, but this type of letting go of revenge flows directly from our understanding of Gospel love, the love Jesus showed on the cross when he asked God to forgive those who were murdering him. Right in the midst of his terrible suffering.

We may discount Jesus' act with an excuse saying, "After all, he was God!" Yet Jesus was human just like us! He knew the feeling of wanting to get even, of taking revenge on those who scorned and crucified him. As the Scriptures note, he could have called forth the heavenly armies and set the scales of justice right.

But again, that's not the way of our God. And revenge, getting even, is not the way of those who seek to model their lives on Jesus' example. God's forgiveness brings us face-to-face with the mystery of God's love and the reality of our own humanness. Using only our own abilities, we would not, could not, forgive as God does. But with God's help (and any help we might receive from the Church community), we can.

Forgiving is not easy. Nor is it always satisfying. But reconciling with our neighbor is the most Godlike thing we can ever do.

> *"The sacrament of Penance can also take place in the framework of a* communal celebration *in which we prepare ourselves together . . . and give thanks together for the forgiveness received. . . ."*
>
> CCC, 1482

Who has hurt us?

Let's pause for a moment in our walk through the mysteries of our faith. Each of the chapters so far have led us forward. We have walked the forest path, stepping over the roots of ancient trees and onto stones made smooth by the tread of many feet; we have stepped carefully onto the glistening stones that provide a sure path over gurgling water. Now we come to a hillside, and the path of stones becomes a path of rocks.

We reach a rock unlike any we met on the forest path or in the bubbling stream. This rock may be shaky and uncomfortable. Perhaps it's covered with rough points and hard to step onto. It might even be one we'd like to step over and ignore. But we do the opposite. We pause awhile. We put both feet firmly in a place on the surface and stop.

Forgiveness given, or forgiveness received, begins with just such a stop. And then we move slowly forward into the way of forgiving or being forgiven.

We invite you to stop now. As you do, think of someone in your life who has hurt you. A husband, a wife, a child, a parent, a grandparent, a close friend, a once-close friend, a neighbor, an in-law child or in-law parent. Who has hurt you?

Be present to the person in your heart. Picture him or her, perhaps at a time when you were both happy and having fun, maybe laughing. Feel your joy at being in good relationship. Think of how precious that person is to God . . . and to you.

Now, consider the hurt; the pain you feel. Can you remove the person from the pain? Pray gently to your God for the ability to do so. Pray gently for the pain to go away and for the person to remain safe in your heart's memory. Pray gently. And when you are ready, step onward.

A Psalm

How wonderful it is, how pleasant,
    for God's people to live together in harmony!
It is like the precious anointing oil running down from
    Aaron's head and beard, down to the collar of his robes.
It is like the dew on Mount Hermon,
    falling on the hills of Zion.
That is where the Lord has promised his blessing—
    life that never ends.

Psalm 133:1–3

"Heartpeace"

elp those of us, O God,
    Who need to listen to the rhythms
      of our heart
    And hunger for the experience
of joy again,
Who just want the hurt and pain to go away
And never return.

In other words,
Help those of us, dear God,
Who need to forgive.

Help those of us, too,
Who need to listen to the rhythms of our hearts
And the struggle with the deeds we've done,
Which hurt both ourselves and others,
Who just want the guilt and pain to go away
And never return.

In other words,
Help us, O God,
Who need to be forgiven.

Amen.

CHAPTER SEVEN

Anointing the Sick—
The Touch That Heals

A wrinkled old skinny hand . . . gently stroked the child's forehead.

"Let's go!" the man yelled. "The bus is coming!" The whole bunch of them climbed on the public vehicle, and the harried mother gave the driver the right amount of change. Then they quickly scanned the interior of the bus and made a dash for the back. The little kids grabbed the window seats, and the adults squeezed in where they could.

As they traveled down the city streets, all of them looked out the windows. The bus would take thirty minutes to get to the home where his mother was being cared for. He hated the thought of seeing her again. It was always so hard.

Yet, he loved her, and, most of the time knew, they were all glad they went—but that was afterward. The actual going remained hard. They could have been doing hundreds of other things, important things. Still, he knew visiting with her was also important. So here they were.

The kids hated the smell of the nursing home. So he had to warn them not to say anything. And they knew the ritual: kiss Grandma, give her a little hug, then sit quietly while mom and dad talked to her. Often he'd said to them, "If she wants to talk with you, she'll let you know. Just behave."

The place smelled as usual. And he glared at the kids. They rounded the corner near her door and there she sat. Tied in a wheelchair. Sound asleep.

This killed him. He knew why they did it—safety and all. "But, God, this is my mom!" he thought. One of the attendants spotted them and came over to move her inside the room. She stirred awake, and spotted little Nanette next to her chair.

"Hi, Meme," the child said. "I came to visit you."

A wrinkled old skinny hand moved slowly toward the child's head and gently stroked the loose strands of hair away from the child's forehead. The gnarled hand then came to rest on the side of the six-year-old's face and gently, gently, stroked her cheek.

Nanette leaned into her grandmother's touch and put her own hand on the sagging, wrinkled skin of the old woman's cheek. Then she gently, gently stroked her Meme.

The scene froze all of them—even the other kids.

And then the moment was gone.

"A particular gift of the Holy Spirit. The first grace of this sacrament is one of strengthening, peace and courage to overcome the difficulties that go with the condition of serious illness or the frailty of old age."

CCC, 1520

As Jesus was walking along, he saw a man who had
been born blind. His disciples asked him, "Teacher,
whose sin caused him to be born blind? Was it his
own or his parents' sin?"

Jesus answered, "His blindness has nothing to do
with his sins or his parents' sins. He is blind so that
God's power might be seen at work in him . . ."

After he said this, Jesus spat on the ground and
made some mud with the spittle; he rubbed the
mud on the man's eyes and told him, "Go and wash
your face. . . . So the man went, washed his face,
and came back seeing.

John 9:1–3, 6–7

_____

*Touch links us as
members of God's
human family.*

_____

Nothing in the world is
like the gentle touch of
another human being.
Shaking hands is a symbol
of affirmation and
agreement. Infants who
are not touched suffer
greatly in their physical
and psychological growth. Elderly people say the one
thing they miss the most is someone touching them.
Toddlers reach for the arms of familiar family members;
we all love to have our backs rubbed. Children enjoy
the security of holding hands.

Touch equalizes us, joins us with another. Between
the touch is energy—the energy of two living beings,
passing one into the other. This can even happen with
our own body.

Place your hands together for a moment and be
present to the touch each hand feels. Sense the energy
flowing between and through your hands.

Touch heals many kinds of hurt. Jesus used touch
to heal people physically. But touch also heals conflict
between us; touch heals prejudice, fear, and pain. Touch
links us and unites us as family, as brothers and sisters
of the world, members of God's human family.

Jesus knew this. Time after time, he reached out to
touch and heal, as he did in the miracle story above.
And what's wonderful about this story is that Jesus
linked earth (the earth created by God) with touch as he
healed the man born blind. Symbolically, Jesus made a
huge circle in this story: the connection between Jesus
as God, Jesus as human, and the earth as part of both
Jesus and the man healed. We are all part of one
another and of Jesus, who is our God made human.

The little girl in our opening story probably didn't go
through a thought process about touching her grandmother. In fact, the grown-ups probably expected her
to say something like "You smell, Gramma." But for
whatever reason that's not what the grandchild said.
Rather, she touched her Meme's cheek.

Children do that; they sometimes startle us with their
holiness. They can teach us so much about life. For
wonderful reasons, the elderly and children have a
mystical union that's obvious all the time. Those of us in
between these two ages may avoid their reality. But the
two extremes of life—the young, the old—bridge the
gap, connect their realities, and sometimes embarrass
the rest of us by finding the truth between each other.

Touching is one of those bridges. Gentle touch gifts
us with the touch of Jesus.

One of the very last accounts we have of Jesus in
the New Testament is when Thomas, an apostle, finally
gets to meet the Risen Lord. And what does Jesus say to
him? "Touch me. Touch me where it hurts."

This sacrament reminds us we are not the Creator, but the creature.

Being human can be wonderful! And what does being human involve? It means that we get sick, have hardening of the arteries, inherit poor eyesight, become bald well before it's fashionable, get tired and cranky, forget people's names, and so forth. For to be human is to also feel the drag of our connectedness to the earth, to feel the limitations of our body and mind, and to experience the difficulties of living with others.

The sacrament now called the Anointing of the Sick is built on the incompleteness and limited nature of our humanity. This sacrament reminds us that we are not the Creator, but the creature. It renders us humble, a wonderful word connected with the same root concept as *humus* (dirt) and *humor* (it's appropriate to laugh, especially at ourselves). Thus God fashioned us as the best possible way to be—human!

Philosophers and theologians argue as to whether this creation, the one we are in, is the best possible one. Are we living in God's first or second draft, or is this the best God can do? Of course, some of us claim that God could have done better. Why, if we had created the universe, we would have left out mosquitoes, sore throats, and the need for sleep. Oh, what we could do with an extra fifty hours or so a week!

But God did what God did and when the basics were done, God said it was very good. And God doesn't lie.

Death and other limits
Every one of us will die someday. We may not want to think about this fact; we may even try to remove ourselves from reminders of death; we may deny our

own aging and mortality. But the day will come on which we will all close our eyes for good.

So we need to live in and accept the truth. A failure to face personal problems, to "stuff them," as some say, does not make them go away. They may appear to

> *Being in touch is a part of living with a healthy spirituality.*

does not make them go away. They may appear to go away if we don't talk or think about them, but they resurface in depression, high blood pressure, or an anger addressed haphazardly to anyone who happens to be around. The truth will set us free. Failure to speak the truth will enslave us in hundreds of ways.

Tuning in to the truth or the pain of our lives is important. Yes, doing this is difficult, but the path of truthfulness is the path to God. Here we experience the value of touch both as a metaphor and as a gesture of healing. We use the phrase "being in touch with reality." We even describe serious mental illness as being out of touch with the real world.

Being in touch with our own feelings, our own gifts, is a part of living with a healthy spirituality. And reaching out to others, even in the advertising slogan "Reach out and touch someone" has a ring of goodness to it. When we become close to others, don't we say that we touch their heart? And the simple touch the child offered to her grandmother in the opening story—wasn't that both a touching of skin and a touching of hearts?

Death is part of life. Lack of an awareness of one's personal death depreciates one's appreciation of life, especially the present, the right now. We have heard of people who have gone right to the door of death only to turn around and be given more time to live. Those people do not return the same as before. They speak of cherishing each moment and of living each day as if it were one's last. They describe ordinary meals as tasting better than anything they had ever eaten. They do not take life for granted; they somehow know that every minute is a gift.

Being reminded of our finite nature, our mortality, our dependence on God, who is the author of life, sobers us and wakes us up to life.

Suffering and sickness

In some ways death is easier to understand than human suffering and sickness. The writers of the Old Testament struggled with these dark aspects of life and brought forth various theories to explain them. Some thought that God punished us for sins by making us suffer. Their theory was: God rewards those who do good; God sends evil on those who do evil. Thus, God balances the scales.

We encounter Job sitting atop a garbage pile.

The Book of Job in the Old Testament deals with the problem of suffering and sickness. Job is a well-to-do landholder who has everything going for him. He has riches, a good marriage, great kids, a fine reputation, and money in the bank.

The author of the Book of Job places a curious conversation in the story, a dialogue between God and someone who is cynical of Job's goodness. "Would Job still be good if he lost everything?" the cynic asks. "Take away his family, his friends, and his riches and then we'll see how good a person Job is!"

God accepts the challenge, and the events of Job's life systematically separate him from all that seemed to make his life happy and successful. Toward the end of the story, we encounter Job at the edge of town, sitting atop a garbage pile. The people passing by cannot resist taking a few minutes to analyze how and why he got where he is. Job listens and mostly disagrees, for he knows both himself and his God.

One passerby says, "Job, you've sinned and you're just getting your just desserts!" (Ah! the philosophy of retribution!) But Job cannot accept this simple explanation, because he can't remember doing anything bad.

Another wayfarer notes that Job must have done something wrong but that he has forgotten about it. (With this system of justice, forgetting does not exempt one from the consequences!) Job doesn't buy this explanation either.

> *The events of Jesus' life ripped dignity from him; his friends abandoned him.*

A third theorist comes by and comforts the man on the garbage pile with the thought that he was, in truth, a good man, but that his ancestors were not and so God is punishing Job for their transgressions. As expected, Job remains unconvinced.

Finally Job takes his case to God and asks for an explanation. God responds by reminding Job that God is God, the Creator of all, and that no one can understand God's wisdom. Job must simply trust what's happening as part of God's sense of what is best. End of story.

Well, not exactly. The final act belongs to Jesus. Job is the innocent one who suffers; and so is Jesus. We cannot resolve why Jesus suffered and died the way he did with an easy or facile explanation. The events of Jesus' life, like those of Job's, ripped dignity from him through the scourging and crown of thorns; his friends abandoned him; and in the poignant scene in the garden, even God appears to pull away from him. Jesus is alone; he is human.

We may think that the Scriptures gives no answer to the problem of suffering and sickness. However, an answer is there; it's just that we do not always find the answer reasonable and comforting. And what is the answer? God knows what is best for us and God would not put us through something God had not experienced as well. In Christ Jesus, God suffered and died for us. And this suffering and death took place on a day that we call "good"—Good Friday.

The healing touch

How does all this connect with the healing stories of Jesus? The Gospels describe Jesus as going about doing good. And part of that goodness was the care and concern he showed others, especially those who were sick, blind, wounded with leprosy, dying, and dead. But Jesus doesn't cure everyone. Is Jesus mixed up? Does Jesus have favorites? The "problem" of suffering and sickness is not easy to solve.

We can, however, make some statements that lead us toward the truth. (1) God loves us all the time. (2) God desires what is best for all of us. (3) God places in creation resources for healing and for bringing health to humanity. (4) God sets in the human heart a desire to heal that which is sick and to alleviate human suffering. (5) We are to use that which God has given us.

The work of healing is a work that Jesus himself undertook. He went about doing good. He reached out to those who where afflicted in body and in mind. He also invited those who came after him to do the same.

The sacrament of the Anointing of the Sick makes present the healing touch of our God. Through the administration of soothing oil onto the body of the recipient, through this touch, the power of God is present—to heal and to bring strength.

That power is now part of the life of the Church. We in the Church participate in the healing ministry of Jesus. Some of us are doctors, nurses, pharmacists, medical researchers. Some of us care for children, spouses, parents, grandparents, friends. All of these works are part of extending Jesus' healing touch to others.

We accept the limitations that are simply part of our being human. We are grateful to God for our life and for all the moments of our life, even those moments in which we suffer. God's love obliges us to help heal others—those close to us and those distant.

Some of us today believe that the earth itself is ailing because of the mistreatment it has received from thoughtless, callous humans. Working to heal the earth, to make our environment more healthy, is also part of God's healing work.

And our relationships may need healing too. Recent learning has given us new wisdom about the complexities of human relationships. Through the wisdom of the helping professions, counseling, and other forms of therapy, we can now move from sickness to health. This, too, is part of healing.

The sacrament of the Anointing of the Sick reminds us of our limitations as humans. But it also alerts us to the God-given power given to the Church community to heal all that is unhealthy and hurt. With God as our model and guide, let us "reach out and touch someone."

> ❧
> *Perhaps the healing was a healing of the soul.*
> ❧

Several major advertisers know exactly how to get to us. They come through our hearts. We get teary eyed just watching heart-wrenching commercials because they touch us in our experience with family and friends. This isn't bad. In fact, for some of us, it's good, because it helps bring to mind our own real-life situations.

The experience and lives of others touch us. This confirms our belonging to one another. The human experience has common thoughts and feelings.

Once again, our God is on top of our needs. This is true of the family in our opening story. God knows that one of the ways God can *touch* us is through the touch from another. We connect with the healing power of God through the healing touch of another.

Sometimes God seems to refuse to heal. However, we see only pieces of the jigsaw puzzle of our life, only part of the pattern of the tapestry. God has the big picture.

And so some of the times we've grown the most, some of the times we've been most challenged in our Christian journey, have been the hard times when we've faced terrible suffering. And perhaps the healing that came was of a different sort than we expected. Perhaps the healing was a healing of the soul. Becoming better persons for having endured the pain.

We encourage you to thank God not only for those times in your life when you needed healing and received it, but for those times when healing, human style, didn't come. Ask God for the strength to get through those times in the future when this will happen. We know our God has a great explanation waiting on the other side of the experience of earth. And sometimes we even feel like saying to our God, "It better be good!"

A Psalm

God heals the broken-hearted and bandages
   their wounds.
Great and mighty is our Lord; his wisdom
   cannot be measured.   *Psalm 147:1, 3–5*

Of Bandages, Lotion, and God

We think, dear God,
   It must certainly be true
   That you were very much involved
      in discovering
The wonderful healing power
Of ordinary bandages

And smooth, slippery lotion.
Because wonderful, magical, mystical, miracles happen
When a scraped knee gets a bandage,
Pressed gently with a little human hug,
And tears are blotted away
With an understanding voice and words.

And because body and mind are made much better
When soothing, warm lotion
From caring hands
Is rubbed gently on a body
Searching and seeking solace
From worldly pressures and discomforts.

And so, dear God, please know
We haven't overlooked
The evidence of your touch of wisdom
In wonderful realities
Like bandages and lotion
Given by someone who cares.
Amen.

CHAPTER EIGHT

Holy Orders—Inviting the Community to Celebrate Life

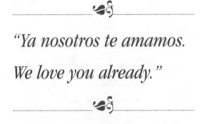

"Ya nosotros te amamos. We love you already."

The young priest knocked on the door, wishing that he'd met his pastor before actually moving in. But he also knew things didn't always work out that way, especially in Hispanic ministry. Everyone knew that there was a shortage of priests, period, and even more so in the Hispanic church. So he just said yes to the assignment with the hope that it'd work out.

Then the door flew open, and Father Conroy was there. "Come in!" he commanded, without even a hello.

"I'm Father Rodriguez, Father," the new priest said.

"I know, I know. I can tell. Come in, come in, I'll show you your room."

Within moments, the young man found himself standing in the center of his new room with the door closing behind him. The pastor had left him alone without a word of welcome! This dumbfounded him. And suddenly he felt both alone and sad.

Then the door flew open again, and he whirled around to see the older priest standing there with his hand still on the doorknob. "Want to come over to the potluck?" he asked. "You could meet the youngsters."

"I'd love to! Just let me put my suitcases in the corner and wash my face and I'll be with you!"

When they entered the hall, resounding applause greeted the young priest as all the faces turned to him. "Bienvenido, Padre! Welcome! Welcome, Padre!" the members of the community called out. "Bueno, es tenerte a ti! Good to have you! Nosotros necesitamos de ti! We need you!" he heard.

Then he realized! This was for him! The older priest had said a potluck, but he meant a welcome! The young priest turned to look at his companion and saw the biggest Irish grin he'd ever seen!

"Aha! I bet you thought I was a real jerk! Ya' know, I couldn't even look you in the eye because I'd give it away! They told me to just get you over here! These families and kids have been planning this for weeks— ever since the diocese announced that *Father Rodriguez* was assigned to our parish And they've been waitin' for two hours! Good thing you weren't any later!"

The young man turned toward the group. "Gracias, amigos! Gracias, gracias. So glad to meet you. Gracias por venir. Thank you for coming. Thank you for the fiesta. Gracias, gracias."

"Gracias, Padre. Es a ti al que le damos gracias. It is you we thank. Es a ti, por lo que le damos Gracias a Dios. It is for you we give thanks to God. Nostros, tenemos oraciones para ti y ahora tu estas aqui. We have prayed for you, and now you are here. Ya nosotros te amamos. We love you already," one of the men said.

Feelings overwhelmed the young priest. Never, ever, had he imagined that this would happen! In his wildest dreams, he had never thought he would feel so welcomed! This made all the anxiety worthwhile. In fact, it probably made everything worth any struggle he'd ever undergone!

And he moved toward his people.

It was now the day before the Passover Festival. Jesus knew that the hour had come for him to leave this world and go to the Father. He had always loved those in the world who were his own, and he loved them to the very end.

Jesus and his disciples were at supper. . . . He rose from the table, . . . tied a towel around his waist . . . Then he poured some water . . . and began to wash the disciples' feet and dry them with the towel. . . . He came to Simon Peter, who said to him, "Are you going to wash my feet, Lord?"

Jesus answered him, "You do not understand now what I am doing, but you will understand later."

Peter declared, "Never at any time will you wash my feet!"

"If I do not wash your feet," Jesus answered, "you will no longer be my disciple."

After Jesus had washed their feet, he . . . returned to his place at the table. "Do you understand what I have just done to you?" he asked. "You call me Teacher and Lord, and it is right that you do so, because that is what I am. I, your Lord and Teacher, have just washed your feet. You, then, should wash one another's feet. I have set an example for you, so that you will do just what I have done for you. I am telling you the truth: no slaves are greater than their master, and no messengers are greater than the one who sent them. Now that you know this truth, how happy you will be if you put it into practice!"

John 13:1-2, 4-8, 12–17

Jesus invites all of us to practice what we preach.

In this gospel story, Jesus gives us a wonderful example of serving one another—a wonderful example of the priesthood. Washing someone's feet is the last thing we'd ever do for our guests once they sat down to our dinner table.

So this ancient practice may be somewhat foreign to us. In fact, it may "gross us out," as we say in our contemporary culture.

But in Jesus' days the feet took a terrible beating. Servants usually refreshed their masters and guests by cleansing their feet when they entered the home, especially before they reclined at the table for a meal.

So when Jesus washes the feet of his disciples, his actions shock them, as we can tell from Peter's reaction. Jesus is taking the role of a servant, a slave! But Jesus does more; he invites and challenges his followers to do the same. "Do as I do," he's saying. "Your attitude must be one of serving those you lead, even to the extreme of the way I serve you." And then Jesus adds, "You will be much happier if you do this!"

Through his actions in this story, Jesus gives all of us (not just those who will be ordained priests) an example. He challenges all of us—as followers and as leaders—to humble ourselves in serving one another. He invites us to be happier!

Jesus invites all of us to practice what we preach. He challenges us to respond to our own "priesthood"—the priesthood of the baptized. Jesus and the Church call all of us to serve, to identify our Spirit-filled gifts, and to use these gifts to the fullest for the good of the universe. God invites us to live as a holy people, led by gifted leaders. And who are these leaders? The ordained priests and deacons, religious men and women, and the members of ordinary holy families.

Our young priest in the opening story is off to a great start. He arrives to serve, and the members of his parish suddenly praise him and give thanks just for his being with them! They are ready to love him. The young priest turns to his people to serve them. So, also, do we need to turn to one another and to our priests.

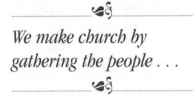

We make church by gathering the people . . .

"The sacraments at the service of communion"—that is how the *Catechism of the Catholic Church* begins its discussion of the sacraments of Holy Orders and Matrimony. The catechism emphasizes service and the creation and support of communion. The word *communion* is a translation of the Latin *communio,* which is at the heart of our present understanding of the Church.

Let's translate all that into ordinary talk. *Communion* means folks getting together. It means being intimate, helping each other live through each and every day, washing each other's feet, eating and drinking together, sharing potlucks, engaging in conversation around the kitchen table, participating in neighborhood garage sales, praying, and singing together. And it also means family.

We make church by gathering the people together to share life and to serve each other. We make church by creating a sense of belonging to each other. In our opening story, the people welcomed their new priest and established instant community—*communio.* They shared life and faith; they created a community—themselves and their priests—so that love could happen.

The sacraments of Holy Orders and Matrimony use the language of creating and supporting church community/family community, but we should not conclude that only those who have received these sacraments are community-makers. Not at all. Countless single people, countless vowed sisters and brothers, live in and work for community.

By calling attention to this aspect of these two sacraments, the new catechism emphasizes that these sacraments are both for the benefit of those who receive them

and also for the benefit of others in the community.
Jesus Christ came to our world for others. So those who
receive these two sacraments must live for others too.
These sacraments are at "the service of communion."

Christian community and leadership

Someone asked, "Who's the leader?" The answer was Peter.

Christianity did not invent
the human organization;
Jesus did not institute the
family. Nor was leadership
the idea of the twelve
apostles. We might say that
community and the need for some form of leadership
are just part of being human. As theologians say, "Grace
builds on nature." Holiness comes from created reality.

Nature provides the foundation for God's activity in
the world. Nature has an inclination, a yearning, for the
coming of God's presence. Why? Because God made
nature this way, just as God put within us a hunger,
a yearning for the more that is God.

The Church began its life with the coming of the
Spirit in the locked room where the disciples cowered.
Most likely when the disciples hit the streets, someone
asked, "Who's the leader?" The answer was Peter. The
apostles knew he was their new leader because Jesus
had singled out their friend both before and after the
resurrection.

The Gospels give us some wonderful stories about
Peter. These reveal that Peter's experiences with Jesus
were far from ideal. The night before Jesus was
crucified, Peter denied him three times. And while the
Gospels mention that the apostle John stood at the foot
of the cross while Jesus suffered and died, they say
nothing about where Peter, the head apostle, was. All
we know is that he was not where the leader of the
future Church should have been!

But like most of us, Peter changed. Soon he took the lead, a position that eventually brought him to Rome, where the Roman emperor had him martyred. According to tradition, Peter felt unworthy to be crucified as Jesus had been, so he asked to be fastened to his cross upside-down!

The Church has always had leaders. Their primary role is to be like Jesus. That is, they are to gather the people, share the Word of God with them, serve them, and celebrate together the sacraments, particularly the Eucharist. Fairly early in the early Church we find the titles the Church uses to describe those who are ordained to holy orders today.

Title One—Bishop: According to the early Church, bishops (the word comes from the Greek *episkopoi,* meaning "overseer" or "supervisor") insured that the teaching of

> *With common belief came common worship.*

the Church in their locale or diocese was truly apostolic. This meant that the teaching expressed what Jesus had said and done. How did the Church know the teachings of Jesus? Through the eyewitness accounts of the apostles.

With common belief came common worship. Thus, bishops presided over the eucharistic liturgy, which we Christians still consider as a symbolic statement of the unity of the Church.

Title Two—Priest: As the years passed after Jesus' death, the Church began to ordain priests. (The word *priest* comes from the Greek word *presbyteros*, which means "elder"; later, the Church added the notion of "presider.") Priests assisted the bishop in his ministry. The Church later added the concept of diocese (a region) and parish (an immediate local community) as its basic geographical divisions.

The role of the priest, like that of the bishop, was centered primarily around the celebration of the sacraments. Priests presided at the Eucharist. But we need to note that their presiding always implied—and implies today—the presence of the community.

The priest does not "say" Mass, while the people only "hear" it. That concept is alien to the Catholic teaching about the Eucharist. All the community—priest and people—celebrate the eucharistic liturgy as well as the other sacraments. Celebration in the Church is a community event, not the act of one person.

The Church centered on the ordained, but not exclusively so.

Title Three—Deacon: Deacons represent the third type of ordained individuals in the Church. (The word *deacon* comes from the Greek *diakonos,* meaning "servant" and, in some places, "the one who waits on tables.") The primary responsibility of deacons is the care of the poor and the needy.

In itself, the fact that the early Church ordained deacons indicates that right from the beginning, the Church had a sense of social justice and a special concern for people who were poor. Deacons assisted the presider (the priest) with the Eucharist and took care of the homeless and the hungry. This ministry actually took on the form of a permanent, lifelong commitment open to married men. The reforms of Vatican II restored the permanent diaconate.

Early on, the Church centered its leadership on the ordained, but not exclusively so. In his letters to the early Christian communities, Saint Paul talked about the many gifts present in the community. No one person had to do everything. Why? Because within any given community, a Christian could find all that was needed to bring vitality to the community.

Church leadership was always meant to take on the quality of service to the whole community. Thus, the Church identified and drew forth from the members of the community their participation and involvement for the good of the whole.

Today, the Church is increasingly aware of the value of shared leadership and shared "ownership." Ordained ministers are to gather the people (especially in prayer and worship) and to ensure that they are informed in their faith. We now speak of leadership by enablement, which means that the Church needs courageous and discerning leaders who know their people and who can call forth from their people greater activity in their Christian life. This applies to all baptized leaders because through baptism all are made participants of the priesthood of Jesus.

Groups, community, and family

Today, the emphasis of the Church is on community, on the connections between all of us. Time after time we have returned to our roots, particularly as they evolved from the first Christian family meal. What was this meal? The Last Supper, which Jesus ate with his apostles on the night before he died.

Through baptism all are participants of the priesthood of Jesus.

The words of Jesus at that gathering (as recorded in John's Gospel) are like the Magna Carta of the Church. Jesus speaks of his oneness with God. He describes his deep love for us and says he will give his life for us. He uses the image of the vine and the branches to show how closely he is connected with us. He blesses the bread and wine and tells his apostles that these gifts are his body and blood. Then he begins to talk about leadership. He doesn't use that word, but his apostles know exactly what he is talking about.

Jesus doesn't simply lecture about leadership. Like a great teacher, he demonstrates what he is talking about. And what does he do to show how the apostles are to lead? He washes the feet of his friends, feet that were no doubt dirty and maybe even smelly. But this act of service is not beneath him. In fact, Jesus' actions embody the kind of leadership that was part of his whole life.

Jesus comes to us as a servant; he empties himself of all divine prerogatives. He becomes the lowest of the low. And he asks his followers to do likewise.

To lead in a Christian way means to lead from behind and to lead from below. Like Jesus.

"The priesthood is ministerial. 'That office . . . which the Lord committed to the pastors of his people, is in the strict sense of the term a service.' "

CCC, 1551

Being family is hard work!

Leadership is one of the gifts God distributes evenly among us. Some of us are called to leadership in our jobs, in our volunteer work, in our neighborhood, in the community (as in politics or Little League or the Scouts). We lead in thousands of ways. However, we often overlook a leadership role most of us play. That is as leaders of a household—no matter what form it may take!

Families represent all kinds of leadership. A newly married couple usually begins with shared leadership. (The equality of men and women is an important aspect of a good healthy marriage.) A home with children may have one or two leaders. Obviously, two can make the work of raising children easier on each, but marriage doesn't always work that way. Sometimes one person bears more of the burden than the other. Sometimes one person takes all the leadership and dominates.

And sometimes a single parent must bear the burden of two. Sometimes a household is made up of a family of grown siblings or grown children still living with a parent. Sometimes a family is one person in a household. But no matter who makes up the family, the ordering of a home takes leadership!

When a new family forms—with marriage or adoption or the birth of a child—the leader has to begin to lead immediately. In the case of marriage or parenting, we don't necessarily have any formal leadership training; we usually just begin to do whatever our parents or those who raised us did.

Sometimes we even decide to do the exact opposite of what our parents did! (We make this decision either consciously or unconsciously.) Most of us can remember little decisions we made as children when we said things like "When I grow up, my kids are going to have whole oranges!" or "When I have kids, I'm going to play with them all the time!"

And then we find ourselves in the reality of family. Someone has to take out the trash! Someone must provide money! Someone needs to get up in the middle of the night with sick kids or pets who need to go out! Someone has to plan the birthdays and insurance coverage and the day to cut the lawn and where each person will sleep, and so on, and so on, and so on!

Being family is hard work! We take good family leadership for granted so much, but it is the core of everything else that happens in our society. Family is the basic cell of both broader society and the larger Church.

We who lead families know how hard this leadership is. We know that we need support and help from institutions (such as the institutional Church, the parish, the diocese, and the rest of the community) so we can lead and be family in the best possible way.

We need support and help from institutions so we can be family.

Many societal leaders have forgotten how their decisions affect families. These leaders—and some of us may be among them— must stop making decisions without considering those affected by them. When making plans that affect family members, leaders need to step into the shoes of the family. They need to stop making so many demands on us. Why? So that we can have time to strengthen our family units; so that we can have time to celebrate being family. When family members have time for one another, our holiness takes root in all of society.

If we are leaders outside the family, we may need to make some changes. If we are priests, religious men or women, or employers in the secular world, we need to consider how what we do or what we do not do affects the family as a system. How can we better support the family's holy work of living each day? How can we eliminate stress and anxiety from the family?

As employers, we need to ask ourselves if the needs of our employees' families are as important as the need to get the work done. We need to remember that our employees bring their family stress and problems and concerns to work with them. So how can we help strengthen these families? How can we create more family-oriented working conditions?

The young priest in our opening story has a long road ahead of him. He, too, must consider how he affects family, how he supports or fragments families. The members of his community are ready for him; they welcome him with love and want him in their midst. Now he must honor that love by loving back, in the same way Jesus did. Families know what washing each other's feet means.

Blessed are those who serve as Jesus did.

A Psalm

Your word is a lamp to guide me
  and a light for my path.
I will keep my solemn promise
  to obey your just instructions.
          Psalm 119:105–6

Ordering the Holy

he coin purse was lost, and it had
        the car keys too.
      Where might it be?
      "We can't go anywhere.
Everyone look!" said Mom.
The teen excavated the garage,
Always a place for buried treasure.
The twins took the upstairs
But got involved with their toys.
So Mom had to remind them of their appointed task.
The little one, only recently mobile on foot,
Followed her mom around the house and into the drawers.
Mom kept one eye on her search and the other on the kids.
Their help needed supervision.
In her mind's eye, she had the blueprints of the house,
So no place was left unsearched for the coins and the keys,
Their resources for survival and escape.

"Say a prayer to Saint Anthony," she yelled
As worry evolved into fear.
"Look everywhere, leave no pillow unturned!"
A smell announced that her little companion needed
    attention.
Into the diaper bag she reached, fully in panic when—
You guessed it!—
Next to the ointment and the small plastic container
    of powder
Was the purse of great price.
"Into the car, kids—we're off for pizza!"
Amen.

CHAPTER NINE
Marriage—Connecting Life with Love

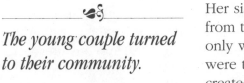

The young couple turned to their community.

Her sister was reading from the pulpit. But the only words Judy heard were the ones that had created so much controversy when she and Jim chose the readings: "Male and female he created them."

Jim thought they should use the other version of the reading from Genesis . . . the one about the rib! This difference of opinion became the focus of long discussions with Father John about the Church's teaching on creation and marriage.

"It was great!" she recalled now. "Who would've thought it'd come to mean so much!"

Suddenly she was jolted out of her thoughts. Father had finished the homily. The moment had come.

Jim was afraid to look at her. All he could hear was the organ blaring; all he could smell was the altar flowers; all he could feel was fear.

Judy was conscious only of the feel of his elbow touching hers. She gazed at the priest without seeing him; all she felt was fear.

"Please join your right hands," the priest said.

Jim turned to see his bride and awe overwhelmed him. Somehow he managed to find her hand, and the gesture felt a little silly because it was like a handshake. Both of them smiled.

She couldn't believe his handsomeness. As soon as he smiled, the expression in his eyes changed from fear to comfort. She knew the love in those eyes.

The world faded away. They turned their heads back to the priest. Everything else was a blur. They were unaware of all the people—family, friends, relatives—who sat behind them, watching.

Then the ceremony was over and they gazed at each other. An end and a beginning! Time passed as in a dream, and then the time had come for them to join the priest in distributing the Eucharist. A simple matter—they'd rehearsed it and knew how because they did it all the time on campus. But they weren't prepared for what happened.

"Jim, the Body of Christ."

"Judy, the Blood of Christ."

The young couple turned to their community.

"Mom, the Body of Christ."

"Gramma, the Blood of Christ."

One by one they served their families and friends. By name, they gave them the Eucharist. And they would never, ever, be the same.

Two days later there was a wedding in the town of Cana in Galilee. Jesus' mother was there, and Jesus and his disciples had also been invited to the wedding. When the wine had given out, Jesus' mother said to him, "They are out of wine."

"You must not tell me what to do," Jesus replied. "My time has not yet come."

Jesus' mother then told the servants, "Do whatever he tells you."

Jesus said to the servants, "Fill these jars with water." They filled them to the brim, and then he told them, "Now draw some water out and take it to the man in charge of the feast." They took him the water, which now had turned into wine, and he tasted it. He did not know where this wine had come from (but, of course, the servants who had drawn out the water knew); so he called the bridegroom and said to him, "Everyone else serves the best wine first, and after the guests have drunk a lot, he serves the ordinary wine. But you have kept the best wine until now!"

Jesus performed this first miracle in Cana in Galilee; there he revealed his glory, and his disciples believed in him.

John 2:1–5, 7–11

The marriage of two ordinary people is a perfect place for Jesus to teach . . .

Virtually all of us have attended a wedding or two. Many of us have attended our own. As the bride or groom, or even as a guest, we want everyone to have a great time at the reception. We generally overspend just to make sure that a good time will be had by one and all!

The marriage reception wasn't any different in the days of Jesus and Mary. Attending a friend's wedding was an ordinary family thing to do. The two of them probably enjoyed themselves dancing, singing, eating, and sharing stories.

Then Mary, as most mothers do, looked around seeing everyone eating and drinking. She probably felt a great surge of compassion for the bride and groom when she realized that the wine was gone. They would be so embarrassed! So she hastened to take care of them and their guests; she knew exactly what to do. (Good leaders of families usually know how to solve problems!)

However, when she approached her son, he wasn't too eager to do as she asked. Perhaps they were having a misunderstanding as parents and children often do. Who knows, but ultimately he did as she said. He loved his mother.

Ordinary events of our lives (like weddings and funerals and birthdays and graduations and even championship Little League games) have within them the potential for miracles.

Obviously, this first miracle was also part of God's plan. Jesus needed to begin somewhere, and God chose one of the best places ever—a wedding! The marriage of two ordinary people is a perfect place for Jesus to teach his disciples important lessons about what is and what is to come.

And what does Jesus teach through his example? He shows that he cares greatly for his mom and he cares greatly about the feelings of his friends.

When God works a miracle through Jesus, the disciples learn something about their God too. This is a God who loves and who wants people to be happy and to celebrate love.

Some of what Jesus was showing at the wedding also happened in our opening story. Ordinary events of our lives (like weddings and funerals and birthdays and graduations and even championship games) have within them the potential for miracles—big and small. These ordinary events are conversion moments.

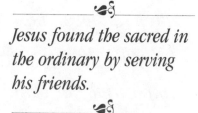

Jesus found the sacred in the ordinary by serving his friends.

We all know about moments in which the sacred shines through the ordinary. The young couple distributing communion at their own wedding experienced that. Serving the Eucharist to their families and friends made them feel the loving presence of God. As they served others they committed themselves to a life of service to each other and to their families and friends. Just as Jesus did: He found the sacred in the ordinary by serving his friends. The opportunity to see a miracle each day, the miracle of love.

"In our own time, in a world often alien and even hostile to faith, believing families are of primary importance as centers of living, radiant faith. For this reason the Second Vatican Council, using an ancient expression, calls the family the Ecclesia domestica. *It is in the bosom of the family that parents are 'by word and example . . . the first heralds of the faith with regard to their children. They should encourage them in the vocation which is proper to each child.' . . . It is here that . . . all members of the family exercise the* priesthood of the baptized. . . ."

CCC, 1656, 1657

The Church considered marriage a sacrament of creation.

Marriage is the last of the seven sacraments that the Church identified. More than a thousand years passed after Jesus' death before the Church listed marriage among the sacraments. Why? Many answer this with an interesting response. The Church, they conjecture, linked marriage to that "bad sex stuff." Perhaps that did have a little to do with not naming marriage as a sacrament for so many years, because the Church did link original sin and sexuality.

But the real reason seems to be that the Church considered marriage a sacrament of creation. Unlike all the other sacraments, marriage traced its history all the way back to that famous garden. In the Book of Genesis, we read that in the beginning, humans were created female and male, in the image of God we were made.

Through a study of the history of the sacraments, we learn that the Church first searched the life of Jesus and the life of the early Church for its sacraments or religious rituals. Because marriage existed before the time of Jesus, the Church thought that while it was sacred (as is everything else in creation), it was not so special that it merited a sacramental label. It was ordinary.

Also, early in its history, the Church began to place a great value on consecrated, or vowed, virginity. The example of Jesus, of course, was an important part of this spiritual tradition. Also, after the Roman persecutions ended at the beginning of the fourth century, martyrdom was no longer the primary way a Christian made a heroic commitment to Jesus. Up to that time, the

Church ascribed sainthood only to martyrs—those who died for their faith.

Very soon, the Church replaced that tradition with an emphasis on consecrated virginity, which the Church valued as the "new" way of heroic sanctity. Roman Catholics gradually began to associate celibacy with the ordained priesthood. And while the Church writers during these early centuries occasionally referred to the importance of marriage, for the most part the Church simply thought of marriage as part of creation and took it for granted.

Marriage and sacramentality

The Church began to value the experience of marital love.

After many, many years of its history, the Church gradually began to think of marriage as a sacramental reality. People began to notice the wonderful joy associated with creating and nurturing children. They noticed that love could grow between a wife and husband.

What gradually happened was that the Church began to value the experience of marital love, especially in the fact that it could provide children. When church leaders searched the Scriptures, they found two readings that captured their attention. The first reading was the wedding feast of Cana with the presence of Jesus and God's working of a miracle to help celebrate the love of the married couple. The second reading was the wonderful text from the letter to the Ephesian community of Christians. In this letter, the epistle writer described marriage as being part of the relationship between Jesus and the Church.

In the Middle Ages (A.D. 700–1400), the Church also became more involved in the legal structures of society.

Soon the Church became the official witness to marriages between Christians. (The Church was involved in marriages earlier, but mostly with people who had special social standing, for instance, the royalty.)

Becoming more involved in weddings and in all their secular ramifications (property and children), the Church became more aware that marriage was something quite special. By the time of the Council of Trent (sixteenth century), the Church officially listed Christian marriage as one of the seven sacraments of the Church community.

Thus, the Church proclaimed the sacramental, or sacred, aspect of marriage. The Church celebrated the fact that marriage is holy and that it has a special role to play in the life of the Church.

The whole of creation is a sign of God's presence, power, and love. The wonders of creation (the song of a bird, the gentle rain on a spring morning, the smile of a child) are signs, or reminders, of God. If we take time to notice creation, we become aware that it is charged with the presence of God. Thus, we become aware of the sacramentality of our universe. That is, through creation we meet God. And marriage has this same kind of sacramentality. In a sacramental marriage we meet Christ.

God is present in the love a couple shares.

Two in one

"And the two shall become one flesh" is a phrase often heard in the marriage ceremony. This phrase originated in the Book of Genesis. The ancient community that first created this text was a community based on the extended family. At that time, people lived in small

In a sacramental marriage we meet God in the love a couple shares.

hamlets and villages. Some were nomads who traveled to wherever they could find food for their livestock.

These ancient peoples connected their marriage customs with what we call "patriarchy," which meant that men ruled and that in marital matters, the family of the groom was primary. A bride, therefore, was taken from her family and was placed in the family of the groom.

If the husband died, the wife did not return to her family of origin. No. She was simply without family ties. As a result, widows were quite vulnerable. For this reason, the care of widows and orphans was a work of special spiritual meaning for God's people.

When describing marriage, the Book of Genesis says that the man shall leave his father and mother and join with his wife. Then the two will become one. A very important point is being made by the Scripture writers: Marriage has deeper social meaning than family; marriage is the closest interpersonal relationship imaginable between adults. It is more important than the relation of a child to his or her mother and father. This also means that, from a religious perspective, the sharing of life between wife and husband is incomparable.

> *These sacred songs describe the holiness of marriage, especially in its sexual aspect.*

One of the most beautiful books of the Bible is the Song of Songs (sometimes called the Canticle of Canticles). For many centuries, Christians interpreted this collection of love poems and songs as referring to the relationship between God and God's people. In other words, the book was an allegory. Readers of the Bible were not to interpret the story literally.

However, all that has changed. Now most biblical scholars agree that these songs about the relationship between a woman and a man were probably wedding songs and they mean just what they say. These sacred songs describe the holiness of marriage, especially in its sexual aspect. The two shall become one.

Christian marriage and Vatican II

The official teaching of the Church for the first half of the twentieth century described the primary goal or meaning of Christian marriage as "the procreation and education of children." When the Catholic Church met to update its teachings at the Second Vatican Council

> *God's love brought forth all of creation; married love brings forth new life.*

(1962–1965), a debate ensued over the way the Church understood Christian marriage. Many of the bishops at the Council felt that the Church's emphasis on procreation and education of children was too one-sided. After all, they argued, the love between the wife and husband was both important and holy.

Thus, when Vatican II articulated its final teaching on marriage, the bishops gave equal weight to two aspects of marriage: (1) the couple's relationship and (2) their openness to bear children (that is, to procreate). The bishops captured the idea in a wonderful way by saying that in Christian marriage the love of the wife and the husband brings forth new life. Love creates life! Just as God's love brought forth all of creation, so married love brings forth new life.

In the couple's love for each other, especially as expressed in loving sexual intercourse, new life comes to be. Thus the two aspects of marriage are not opposites; they do not contradict each other. They are, instead, the two sides of a single coin: marital love in its fullest expression.

Another dimension of marriage that is part of its sacramentality is that the relationship is one of fidelity (faithfulness); it is a lifelong relationship. The Church has come to appreciate marital fidelity as a sign of God's fidelity to us. Just as God has entered with us into a covenantal relationship marked by steadfastness and commitment without end, so does the covenant of marriage, in its way, mirror this aspect of God.

The love of God enters into human love, blessing it and sanctifying it. Marriage becomes a Christian "vocation" in its own right. Marriage focuses God's invitation to love. Thus, we love our spouse, our children, our global community.

The family is one of God's very best ideas!

> *"Christ chose to be born and grow up in the bosom of the holy family of Joseph and Mary. The Church is nothing other than 'the family of God.'"*
>
> CCC, 1655

Do we strengthen and affirm our married families?

As a people, we need from the Church more than schools for educating our young and buildings for celebrating the sacraments. We need the support and encouragement of one another. Thus, a wonderful thing happened in our American Catholic Church in 1979: Our bishops and others named 1980 as "The Year of the Family" and the 1980s as "The Decade of the Family."

Then the Church released a pioneering document to help family members. *The Plan of Pastoral Action for Family Ministry* spelled out specific ways we as church can help ourselves through ministry with hurting families, with the separated or divorced, with leadership, with developing families, with parents, and with the married (including those seeking marriage.) The document offered a definitive plan to reach out and include, to minister with and celebrate those groups within our community whom the Church may have neglected in the past. In this type of ministry, we, as church, strengthen our community by strengthening our members and our families—our most precious community.

All over our country, dioceses and parishes formed marriage preparation policies after the publication of the pastoral plan. Formerly, only the priest prepared couples. Now, couples prepare longer before they marry and fulfill specific steps, such as meeting with experienced married couples who help those wishing to marry to look at marriage as it really is, in practice. The older married couple, wise in the issues that married couples encounter, help the young woman and man seeking marriage to discuss important issues and to work them out before the wedding date.

We'll probably never know how much of a difference all this makes. But what is wonderful in this "peer ministry" (married couples helping those who are seeking marriage) is that we who are married help prepare our own for the sacrament of Matrimony. Those who work in this ministry have learned a great deal about premarriage and postmarriage realities. And what is learned is extremely important to and for the Church.

We know, for example, that we as church need to put even greater effort (people, time, and money) into this vital ministry. Real marriage preparation begins in early childhood (when we experience the marriages around us) and continues as we build expectations and make decisions about our own hoped-for marriage. Because of this fact, we might consider doing more for children, most of whom will eventually marry. We might ask ourselves—do we revere and honor this key sacrament, which is a daily celebration and image of Jesus' love for all the rest of us? Do we strengthen and affirm our married families?

And if we're married, are we living the sacrament of Matrimony? Does our daily, ordinary married life invite and challenge us to be more loving for one another? Do we do all (or some or most!) of those big and little everyday things that say "You are precious to me"? Do we let the one who loves us really love us? We all know the old saying, "Love isn't love till it's given away." And love cannot be given if it isn't accepted (without criticism nor expectation of any more than what is given).

Those of us who aren't married need to ask ourselves if we encourage those who are married by praising and affirming them when we experience the evidence of their love. When we see their sacramentality at work, do we tell them?

Perhaps today you'll have either the chance to strengthen your own union or that of someone else. We invite you to take the risk; support one another for the good of all of us.

"We must also remember the great number of single persons who, because of the particular circumstances in which they have to live—often not of their choosing— are especially close to Jesus' heart and therefore deserve the special affection and active solicitude of the Church, especially of pastors."

CCC, 1658

A Psalm

We put our hope in God;
    our protector and our help.
We are glad because of God;
    we trust God's holy name.
May your constant love be with us, O God,
    as we put our hope in you.

Psalm 33:20–22

Help Us Hope, Lord Jesus

 We pray today, Lord,
For those who are married,
For those who were once married,
For those who will one day marry,
And for those who will never marry.

That's all of us, Lord.

We pray for ourselves
Because in the secrets of our hearts
You know our needs.

Some of us are in pain and need your healing touch.
Be with us, Lord, as we find you
In the help of others and one another.

Some of us are joyful, Lord.
Be with us, too, as we discover more of you
In the joy of one another
Or even the joy of you
In self.

But all of us, Lord,
Seek your blessings on our marriages
Or those we love.
For it is in being blessed by you
That we are blessed by one another.
Amen.